THE SATURDAY EVENING POST

Reflections of a Decade

1901-1910

THE SATURDAY EVENING POST
Reflections of a Decade
The First of a Series

1901-1910

THE CURTIS PUBLISHING COMPANY
INDIANAPOLIS, INDIANA

*¶There are two ways of spreading light:
To be the candle or
The mirror that reflects it.*

Edith Wharton 1862-1937

*Reflections of a Decade
1901-1910*

President, The Curtis Book Division
Jack Merritt

Managing Editor
Jacquelyn S. Sibert
Assistant Editor
Amy L. Clark
Editorial Assistant
Melinda A. Dunlevy

Art Editor/Designer
Caroline M. Capehart
Art Director/Designer
Jinny Sauer Hoffman
Associate Designer
Pamela G. Starkey
Art Assistant
Melinda A. Dunlevy

Production Manager
David M. Price
Technical Director
Greg Vanzo
Compositors
Patricia Stricker, Penny Allison

Research Assistant
Danial M. Clark
Proofreader
Kathy Simpson

Table of Contents

The World

New Developments

Introduction

❝In the new century nothing must be impossible.
April 26, 1902, Post

Americans grew accustomed to constant change in women's fashions. Changes in their roles, though, took getting used to.

Americans are used to change. True, should they recognize it as such, they may resist it. It's against human nature to readily accept change. But, so much a part of American history, indeed American life, is it, that oftentimes it is not recognizable.

The years 1901 through 1910, like every period of American history, were dominated by change. But in this first decade of the Twentieth Century, change took on new dimensions and impetus, permeating nearly every aspect of American life.

Rigid social mores loosened after the death of England's Queen Victoria, producing a bolder American. A time of tendency toward large families became a time, as well, of tendency toward divorce.

And, along with the bolder American, in general, came the bolder American woman, in particular—her growing independence evidenced in more daring styles of clothing. By 1905, a hitherto inconceivable bathing costume could be seen frequenting the beaches: "Dark blue or black, made with a skirt, long sleeves and high neck, and worn with a narrow linen collar," this, along with a sunbonnet, gloves, stockings, shoes and oftentimes a veil (to protect the complexion) comprised bold attire for the period.

Bolder still was the new "peek-a-boo" waist and sheath gown. "The sheath gown uncovers a multitude of shins" became a favorite

A declaration of independence.

remark, while "renaissance sleeve," "shirt-waist" and "Alice blue" (after the President's eldest daughter) became regulars in American prose and conversation.

Probably no facet of American living has exceeded the world of women's fashions in rate of growth and change. This, coupled with the strong emphasis placed on style in the 1900s, made fashion a favorite target for editorial quips and jokes.

When life-sized birds and feathers adorned the latest millinery designs in 1907, the following verse appeared in a popular periodical:

We have the horseless carriage,
The wireless and all that,
Also the loveless marriage,
But not the birdless hat.

Wit with words was not restricted to fads in fashion, however. The ping-pong craze prompted this from an editor-turned-poet of the Philadelphia *Bulletin*:

I know I must be wrong,
But I cannot love ping-
    pong.
I cannot sing
In praise of ping;
I have no song
    for pong.

Of course, it wasn't all limericks and light verse for the journalist of the decade. America had barely rung out the old decade when tragedy struck the new: President McKinley was assassinated while attending the Pan-American Exposition in Buffalo, New York.

Some birds became endangered, as many of their species were stuffed and perched atop ladies' hats.

The year was 1901 and the bewildered young vice-president, Teddy Roosevelt, stepped up to face mounting national problems.

Most of these problems were dealt with by *The Saturday Evening Post* at the time, and are, therefore, discussed in this volume. Others, like the Cuban problem, were not covered by the *Post*, but, because of their impact upon the decade, are mentioned here:

At the time Roosevelt became president, America's rule extended beyond her borders to the volatile island of Cuba. Resentful of authority, the island country staged numerous uprisings before regaining independence in 1902.

Meanwhile, within her borders, the great "melting pot" seemed dangerously close to overflowing, as hopeful immigrants came in record numbers to the land of the wide, open spaces in search of "the good life." What they found instead was menial labor (at best) in overcrowded cities. *The Jungle* by Upton Sinclair, published in 1906, exposed the plight of the immigrant and stimulated wide-scale social reform, a result of which was the formation of the NAACP (National Association for the Advancement of Colored People) in 1909.

Corruption in politics and big business was widespread, keeping "muckrakers" well supplied with exposé material. And the Panic of 1907, remedied by J.P. Morgan and his millions, still managed to give the economy a sizable jolt.

Though the problems persisted, change, as the un-

dercurrent of American culture, produced important technological gains, which helped tip the scale toward national optimism.

Between the years 1901 and 1910, the U.S. Patent and Trademark Office assigned a total of 315,193 patents to inventions ranging from aeroplanes to wax pencils dubbed "Crayolas." And a period of tremendous national development became also a period of mounting national pride.

The St. Louis Exposition of 1904 was a celebration of the technologicial strides made thus far, and an anticipation of those yet to come.

An incident which occurred there perhaps best illustrates the rationale of Americans throughout the decade: An ice cream vendor ran out of dishes. Insignificant, perhaps, but rather than pack up and go home he conspired with the nearby Persian waffle maker. . .and created the first ice cream cone.

Typically American. Development initiated by the need for change. Add the element of freedom to act on that need, and you've got the natural progression by which anything is possible.

                        The Editors

Problems and progress of a decade are good cause for reflection.

Daily Living

❧ *Clothes are cheaper, but food is dearer, while education is free. So here, at last, are the conditions of a good appearance, plain living and high thinking—but, alas! philosophers are scarce. (1902).*

Gospel of Privacy

An EDITORIAL

By 1900, progress was already exciting rapid change. Neighbors would soon be minutes, not miles, apart—a prospect which created renewed interest in privacy.

———————————

One reason why no one has written the standard book upon American customs and manners, and a possible explanation why we wait vainly for the Great American Novel, is the fact that American life is in such a constant condition of change.

If one were so gifted as to catch a truly accurate picture of the nation this year, one would find that the next year it was completely out of date and untrustworthy.

This refers not so much to conditions of commercial prosperity or to fluctuations of political feeling as to the small ways of daily life. Never has there been, before, in the history of the world, a country where individuals and whole communities have been so full of the passion for self-improvement as we are today.

Among the ideas which we have half got hold of, and which we are likely to take up with increasing enthusiasm within the next few years, is that of the advantages and delights of privacy. Up to now, we have been domestic without being especially private.

We never make much of a point of pulling the curtains at nightfall across our sitting and dining room windows, and when we first possessed piano lamps with broad umbrella shades we put them at once into the front bay-windows so that the passers-by might also enjoy them.

Formerly we delighted to crowd summer hotels, and the nearer our chairs stood to the chairs of our fellow-guests the happier we were. (If there is a trace of exaggeration in all this the reader will perhaps pardon it, because it serves to heighten a contrast.)

Nowadays each of us longs for a cottage in the country where he may plant his own vine and fig-tree. We screen our front porches with flowers and awnings.

Soon it may happen that some one will rescue the back yard and make of it a pleasant garden. Slight as the evidences of it are, the change is begun. But then, in America, that is almost the same thing as completed. (1902) 🐚

Screening out sunlight by day, protecting privacy by night.

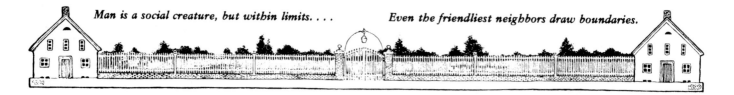

Man is a social creature, but within limits. . . .   Even the friendliest neighbors draw boundaries.

Bachelors in New York

By ROBERT SHACKLETON

The last Census showed that there were in the whole country 5,427,767 bachelors against 3,224,494 spinsters—an excess of 68 per cent of bachelors over the unmarried women. (1902)

In New York City, so it is estimated, there are some 10,000 men who live in bachelor apartments. In the term "bachelor apartments," I am speaking only of those whose home is of more than one room and of those who live in the distinctively bachelor apartment buildings.

From four hundred to four thousand dollars a year—that may in a general way express the range of cost for the one item of rent of a bachelor apartment. It used to be said by many a young man in New York that he could not afford to be married. Now there is many a young man who thinks that he cannot afford to be a bachelor. For when to the rent of an expensive apartment is added the general cost of living that goes with an expensive house—the cost of eating, of clothes, of entertainment, of service, of tips, of theatres—such a total is reached that it need not be a matter of surprise that many a man turns to matrimony for reasons economical.

Between Forty-second and Twenty-third Streets to the north and south, and between Madison and Sixth Avenues to the east and west, may be said, in a general way, to lie the bachelor apartment houses.

Bachelors like to live in the centre of things: of life, of theatres, of amusement. For them the suburbs have no charms; for them the commuter sounds the praises of the country in vain. Within touch of the clubs and theatres and hotels and of the busy life of Broadway and Fifth Avenue the average bachelor must be.

New York, New York! Within her walls in 1907 dwelt many a bachelor in relative luxury.

There are large bachelor houses and there are small; there are buildings which tower far upward, with story piled upon story, and which contain from a hundred and twenty-five to a hundred and fifty suites, and there are other buildings of but four or five stories and which house not more than from fifteen to twenty-five men.

For the average bachelor, strange to discover, is a man who, though anxious to make a gallant show, is not oblivious to possibilities of money saving. But in most bachelor houses there is no outward and visible sign of money saving. Granite-pillared entrances, lobbies ringed round with massive columns, hallways marble-walled and rich-tiled: it is through such as these that many a bachelor goes to his apartments. Dining-rooms there are with oval ceilings of multicolored glass through which the sunlight shines subdued, and in some rooms there is a soft glow that comes from hidden electric lights. One may not dispute the truth of the assertion that it is not good for man to be alone, and yet there is many a New York bachelor who somehow seems to get on more than comfortably.

There is not in New York, as yet, the charm that goes with the chambers where bachelors dwell in some Old-World cities. In New York the tendency is all for newness, and seldom is a building allowed to stand long enough to acquire the gray atmosphere of age. Buildings are cut off in their youth.

But the bachelor homes of New York can show —and this, to the New York bachelor, is the important point—conveniences and luxuries far beyond those of Old-World bachelor houses. Elevators run

only haunt the curio shops of New York, but ransack the colonial homes of Massachusetts, of Maryland, of Virginia. With some bachelors, however, it is not necessary that the furniture be really old; with them it is not at all needful that the furniture be of an earlier manufacture than last year's; but it must be of old design. There is another feature, which, though not so general as those of fireplaces and furniture, is quite common. That is the presence of ancient weapons, of swords and spears, of shields and bows and arrows, of ancient muskets and matchlocks. It is another case of "the arms and the man."

An average rent for an apartment in one of the modern bachelor houses is twelve hundred dollars a year. The bachelor may decrease his expenses by sharing his apartment with another bachelor, but he who wishes the really independent bachelor life, in a way such as will allow him to maintain what the average bachelor of standing considers an adequate station, will spend for rent at least the figure just named.

The greater number of apartments consist of a sitting-room, a bedroom, and a bath. In many cases the sitting room is overfurnished. The bachelor is apt to put in too many knickknacks, too much furniture; he is apt to pack his mantelpiece so closely that he can find no place there for an additional statuette or photograph. It is not unfair to say that the aspect of a bachelor's apartment is all too liable to be what in homely phrase is known as "cluttery." It needs the touch of a woman—but the bachelor will be the last to acknowledge it.

And the sitting-room, though not large, is usually of comfortable size, and so, too, is the adjoining bedroom. The bathroom is shiny in its display of white tiles and porcelain tub and an array of nickeled pipes.

There is much that goes with such an apartment. The rooms are heated and lighted without expense to the

throughout the night; steam heat warms the rooms in winter and ventilating appliances cool them in summer; electric light is in every room; in a few buildings there is even a cold-storage attachment for every tenant, operated by an apparatus in the basement, and giving to each bachelor the opportunity to have bottles or game, icy cold, ready to his hand. For modern comfort the New York bachelor is content to forego picturesque associations.

A notable characteristic of New York bachelor apartments is the fireplace. The bachelor seems to look on that as a necessary adjunct to his home, and therefore in the great majority of bachelor apartments it is in marked evidence. A cheerful glow it makes and serves to give to the bachelor a sense of homelike coziness.

Another characteristic is also marked—the love for furniture of old-fashioned design. The average bachelor with money to spend is sure to spend a great deal of it on furniture of antique pattern. Some put great sums into this, and not

No bachelor apartment was complete without a fireplace and its ornate mantel covered with knickknacks.

tenant, and the house service is without additional cost. Everything, in fact, is seen to for the lone, lorn man. He has none of the cares of housekeeping. For him the servant problem is solved.

For an expense of from eight to twelve dollars a month he even has the personal services of a house valet, probably a soft-slippered, soft-voiced Japanese, who brushes his hat, polishes his shoes, creases his trousers and presses his coat; who never is in the way when not wanted and who is never absent when needed.

The bachelor even finds that his laundry is sent out; and it comes back and is put away in his chiffonier. There is no house laundry, and so this is an outside expense. The bachelor has all the delights of a house-keeping life with far fewer cares. "It is no longer necessary for a man to be married in order to be well taken care of," said one of them to me recently.

The better houses have telephone connections throughout the house (some, indeed, have local and long-distance telephones in each apartment), and breakfast or other meals may at any time be ordered in one's own rooms. For this there is a slight additional expense.

Luncheon and dinner are usually eaten somewhere else than in the bachelor building—the luncheon, hastily, near the man's office, and the dinner at one of the hotels or clubs—for the New York bachelor is a devoted club and hotel man.

In the more splendid apartments—those of six or eight rooms—fine dinners and entertainments are often given. The silverware and china are in some cases furnished by the bachelor himself from his rich-stored closet, and his own personal servants aid in caring for the guests.

In other cases the table furnishings are from the caterer who provides the dinner. Perhaps the dinner

The bachelor, a "regular" at hotel and club restaurants.

is served from the kitchen of the apartment house; still more likely, however, it is served by one of the great catering firms of the city, and in this case it is matter for careful planning to have each course of a long dinner waiting at the apartment door in proper time and order.

At the greater dinners it is not unusual to have some special feature of interest, such as (copying a picturesque old-time dinner achievement) the bringing in of an enormous pastry, from which, when cut, there steps forth a little dancing girl, who there-upon skips fantastically about the table to the applause of the delighted guests.

There have to be very strict rules in bachelor-apartment houses, and there are apt to be a few men in any large house who would like to break those rules; so at times it is necessary for the management to exercise both firmness and tact. Bachelors do not enjoy the wild freedom of life that many picture for them.

Yet, many a bachelor acquires a tenacity of love for his home; a love and affection that, one might think, would come only when the ties of a family are added.

A curious feature of bachelor life in New York is that in some quarters there is a strong dislike of that class of tenants, and that some large apartment houses, constructed especially for bachelors, have been turned into apartments for families.

But, there is only one way of doing away with bachelor apartments: doing away with the bachelors themselves; and so many of the tenants are far past their youth, and thus confirmed in their single life by many years of it, that to change them from bachelorhood seems impossible.

Still, it was a supposedly confirmed bachelor who quaintly remarked that though he declared he would die a bachelor, he did not think he should live till he were married. (1902)

Mastering The Art of Conversation

By WILLIAM MATHEWS

Conversational skill is a valuable asset, especially where it pertains to the art of persuasion.

William Mathews was a former Professor of Rhetoric for the University of Chicago.

H ow is it that the actual decisions and determinations of men in the grave matters of life are brought about? Is it by the play of oratorical artillery—by conviction through public debate? No; it is by the hand-to-hand encounter of private conversations.

Assuming, then, that there is an art of conversation, the mastery of which requires study and practice, the question arises: How shall skill in this art be acquired? To answer this question we must first determine what are the qualifications essential to a good converser. First, there is the physical quality of *a pleasing voice*, always calm, quiet and low.

Of the mental conditions of good conversation the most important is *knowledge*. Knowledge may be acquired, of course, by books or by observation.

But to be a good talker one requires not only to have a varied knowledge, but to have it *at his instant and absolute disposal*. All his acquisitions from books, observations or converse with others should, therefore, be thoroughly digested so as to be at the very tip of his tongue.

A fund of piquant and amusing *anecdote* is helpful in conversation, and serves to break its monotony or diversify it when it falls into a groove or rut.

Modesty and *simplicity* will add greatly to the charm of anyone's conversation, and it is almost needless to say that *unselfishness* is essential to all good conversation. Who that has once heard him can ever forget the man who monopolizes the attention of the social circle, and insists on keeping others waiting till he has "said his say."

Yet, of all the qualities needful to a good converser, none is more indispensable than *tact*—a gift which defies exact definition, but which all recognize when they see it. It springs from a union of mental quickness and lively sympathy. Born in some persons, it is by others never acquired. The man who has this gift knows that a thorough discussion of a subject is out of place in a conversation and drops it the moment he discovers that its interest has been exhausted.

Of all the qualifications for social converse which we have named, is there one, except possibly the last in some exceptional cases, which may not be possessed by any man of fair abilities who will take a reasonable amount of pains? Conversation is an art; but it is an art which may be acquired. The best talkers, like the leading adepts in any other art, were born with peculiar gifts; but their aptitude was cultivated by reading, reflection and observation, and especially by frequent and varied practice. In short, the way to learn to talk is—to talk. (1902)

Letters to Women in Love

By MRS. JOHN VAN VORST

I

To Miss Beatrice Thayer, Fifth Avenue, New York.

My dear Beatrice:

You know how fond I was of your dear mother, and that, since her death, I have looked upon you as a sister. In any case I take the liberty of occupying myself about you, as though you had turned to me for protection!

You can imagine my surprise on receiving from Reginald Wells a long, long letter—all about you!

Reginald Wells loves you. Of course, this you knew. And Reginald does not want you as a friend! What shall he do?

II

To the same:

You are young, pretty, charming, cultivated. What more natural than that you should be loved, and fall in love yourself? Yet the mere indirect suggestion of such a thing brings an outburst.

III

To the same:

Last night the maid brought me your telegram.

You don't declare that you will never marry him. If he really loves you, he must wait.

IV

To the same:

Indignant, enraged, discouraged, petulant, thus you appear in your last letter. And why?

Simply because Reggie has proposed to you! What a terrible offense indeed!

V

To the same:

You seem perfectly amazed that Reggie should not have written to you since landing in America. Why should he write to you?

VI

To the same:

I send this to your New York address. Your ship ought to get in to-day. Let me hear from you as soon as possible after arriving. Is it to be, or not to be?

P.S. Your telegram just arrived. Heartiest congratulations to you both. Don't make a too long engagement! Your father must be in a hurry to have such a son-in-law as Reginald. Write soon and remember I love you both as much in your foolish happiness as I did in your foolish misery! (1903)

From the Frying Pan to the Fire

From ADAM AND EVE ON DOWN

Good Ship Matrimony

An EDITORIAL

The population figures gathered by the new Census are now complete. It appears that the males have largely the advantage, outnumbering the gentler sex 24 in every 1,000. The figures show about three-fifths of the people of the country (including children) are single, a third are married, and a small fraction of one per cent are divorced. (1902)

A good many people laughed at a Chicago man when he began to collect statistics to discover the relation between divorce and bad cooking. But they laugh no longer; for the ingenious Chicagoan has shown from the local records that in no less than one-fourth the divorce cases in a given period the avowed cause was the wife's cookery.

These wonderful facts call attention to the low state in which the art of housekeeping still lingers—not in Chicago alone, but wherever the free flag floats.

One of the curses of our imperfect, unformed though forming civilization is a certain uppishness that makes men and women foolishly discontented, that makes them talk and think much on false and silly ideas of their own dignity and deserts. This curse is a passing matter, doubtless inevitable; but it is serious while it lasts. It makes men careless at their work; it makes women care-

The keeper of the house— by no means just a housewife.

less at theirs. The man is peevish because he has a twenty-five-dollar-a-week job instead of the presidency of the company. The woman is fretful because she has to help or do her own work instead of spattering mud on the masses from the wheels of her own chariot. The men are kept in order somewhat because they have an unfeeling employer over them; but the women are not thus monitored, are free to give way to their discontent—and they, being human, do give way.

Hence this general tilting of feminine noses and curling of feminine lips at such "vulgar" things as housekeeping. Yet there is not anywhere in organized society an occupation that can absorb more intelligence, skill, energy and patience than housekeeping. Perhaps that's why men discreetly leave it in the hands of the women. But is it not strange that they do not rise more rapidly to their opportunities, that they do not develop the great science and art which the world looks to them to elevate and improve? Is it not a reproach to any woman that a mere restaurant can set a better table than she can, that any mere hotel can be more comfortable, better ordered, better cleaned and dusted than her house?

The true theory of marriage is a partnership on equal terms for a safe and comfortable journey through a world in which the ideal is hard and fast inclosed in a bristling burr of the material. To this partnership the man gives his ability as an income-getter, the woman her ability as a home-maker. On the good ship Matrimony not husband or wife is captain and pilot, but Love; and husband and wife are his hard-working crew; and if they don't work, each at the equally important duties, smash goes the ship on the rocks.

If the average woman worked as many hours each day at her housekeeping—thinking, doing and superintending—as her husband thinks he works at income-getting, there would be cobwebs on the divorce calendars, and, thanks to the women, men and women would be marching forward to the millennium quickstep.

It is important that men educate themselves. It is more important that the women, the mothers and counselors and inspirers of men, educate themselves—in that only true education which teaches that as the secret of the mystery of the universe lies hid in the "flower in the crannied wall," so does the mystery of progress and happiness lie hid in the small, homely things which the ignorant call trivial and vulgar. (1903) 🐾

Ruin by Women

An EDITORIAL

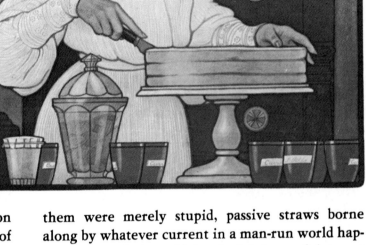

Blaming the women has been a popular masculine consolation since Adam's time. "I was ruined by women," said a male citizen some time ago as he was about to leave for the penitentiary. He meant that he left his home and stole his bank's money to riot with females, a majority of whom would have been quietly at work in some productive occupation if economic conditions—that are made exclusively for men—had given them a fair chance. Nearly all of them were merely stupid, passive straws borne along by whatever current in a man-run world happened to catch them. If they hadn't been of that sort they wouldn't have been rioting.

Probably four-fifths of the initiative and of effective power are in the hands of men. This is true of society and of most individual cases. If the modern well-to-do woman is more ornamental than useful it is because that status was fixed for her by her father and husband. Men deplore that women brought up in easy circumstances consume much and produce little. Many of the men who deplore it loudest would perish of chagrin if the neighbors should know that their own wives were doing the family washing to save expense. Among the well-to-do, the wife is the token of the husband's gentility. He bemoans the cost, but is secretly delighted to be the husband of a "lady."

We write this in the interests of conservation. A prodigious amount of thought that might produce good social steam wastes itself in mere vapor over the ruin wrought by women. We do not recall a single case, from Adam and Samson down, where a man really up to his job was ruined by a woman. (1910) 🐾

Are We Spoiling Our Children?

Cheating the Children

An EDITORIAL

One of our multi-millionaires who began life as a poor lad and did not succeed until middle age is said to enjoy the fun and luxury which his money brings him like a hot-headed boy. He goes to balls and the play incessantly; he buys pictures, yachts, automobiles, and exults and rejoices loudly in each, until he becomes a bore to his blase companions.

"How can you find so much pleasure in such things?" one of them asked him the other day.

"Because they are new to me. Remember that I had nothing when I was a boy," he answered.

Isn't there a significant hint here to well-to-do

This small newsboy, damp and shivering in the cold for hours, should, in theory, have much enjoyment awaiting him in the maturity of his old age.

American parents of to-day? They are cheating their children's lives of certain enjoyments which rightfully belong to their mature age by forcing them upon them almost in their cradles.

Two generations ago the respectable, God-fearing father and mother in this country believed that the first virtue to teach their children was self-sacrifice. "Spare the rod and spoil the child" was their maxim. The rod was not spared to the child, and the boy, as a rule, was forced to work hard for his education or living. Money was scarce in those days, and the root idea of religion was asceticism.

And what do we teach our children now? We have gone to the other extreme in our treatment of children. Money is plenty. The "old man" has heaped up enough for his boys and girls. He stuffs them with luxuries, he roasts them in the fire of his prosperity, just as live geese in Strasburg are stuffed and roasted—and with very much the same result to their brains and hearts.

Other nations were wiser. The heir to an English dukedom is kept in the nursery until he is old enough to go to Eton and be thumped and mauled by other boys. A royal princess of ten eats boiled mutton and pudding with her governess at noon, and wears clothes as simple as those of any farmer's child. They never hear of "Society," although they are being trained to rule over it.

The child of the wealthy American at two years old is probably a competitor in a Baby Show at Asbury Park, arrayed in satin and lace and stared at by thousands. Or if her parents are a little too well-bred for that they take her to hotels in summer or scamper over Europe with her until she is grown. She is, as a rule, over-dressed and self-conscious. She has at twelve the jewels, the manners and the effrontery of a middle-aged woman.

In all our large towns the children of wealthy parents have their theatre and card parties, their cotillons and balls, for which lit-

Deprived is the youngster surrounded by comfort and playthings.

tle boys engage their partners days in advance, and provide them with bouquets of costly roses. Their talk is of flirtations and engagements—a feeble parody of the feeble doings of their elders.

Now, is this state of things fair to the boys and girls?

At ten they are cheated out of the fun of childish games, out of the relish for plain food, out of the joyous ignorance, the dreams, the innocence which belong to childhood; and at thirty they are cheated out of all enjoyment or the pleasures of middle age because they were satiated with them when they wore kilts. (1903) 🐦

Wholesome Neglect
By WILLIAM MATHEWS

A great Swedish statesman once said that the world is governed too much. Whether true or not of states, the *mot* is certainly true, in many cases, of children. How often has a bright boy, full of life and energy, been spoiled by the very efforts—conscientious, painstaking, but incessant, over-anxious, fussy—of his parents or tutors to train him well! In their anxiety to make him a model of virtue, they allow him hardly any freedom or oppor-

tunity to do wrong, and, being kept continually in leading-strings, unexposed to temptations, the triumphant conflict with which would teach him self-reliance and strengthen his moral backbone, he becomes a moral weakling. Boys thus stuffed with advice, and fettered in their action, resemble a boy rightly reared no more than a chicken trussed on a spit resembles a fowl in the field.

Some parents do not seem to know that there is such a thing as wearing out the conscience of a child by extreme pressure and overstimulation. "I have known a child," says Sir Henry Taylor in his very suggestive *Notes on Life*, "to have a conscience of such extraordinary and premature sensibility, that at seven years of age she would be made ill by a remorse for a small fault. She was brought up by persons of excellent understanding, with infinite care and affection, and yet, by the time she was twenty years of age, she had next to no conscience and a hard heart." We could name several noted skeptics of the day—disbelievers in Christianity—whose fathers were clergymen that held in this age of progress to a rigid, ultra-conservative type of theology. How true is it that, as that wise wit and witty divine, Dr. Thomas Fuller says, "People who lace their bodies too tightly are apt to grow awry on one side!" A shrewd old English lady was once asked what she would recommend in the case of children who had been too carefully educated. She replied: "A little wholesome neglect." (1902) 🐦

Our Ill-Bred Guests

By LILIAN BELL

Many magazines fling wide their portals to every sort of preachment destined to educate women in courtesy, unselfishness, domestic accomplishments and attractive wiles to ensnare the hearts of men; but if very much advice is given to young men, telling them how to become truly popular, instead of merely being invited everywhere—how really to be liked instead of merely to think they are liked—it has not come under my eyes.

Most men don't care to know the difference. They are quite content with scores of invitations, with smiles of welcome and with the knowledge that they are sure to be invited when anything big is on. These men are neither sensitive nor very observing.

But there is a small class of thinking men, who do not belong to this generalization, who notice that they are only invited to the big crushes, and that when the small, select affairs are on their names are off. These men want to know why, and, not being able to see why, they fall into the general category of those who accuse women of being false, artificial, insincere, and of playing a part.

That may all be true, but it is not the answer to the question of why certain very good-looking, well-educated, well-groomed men are not really liked by women who entertain and who make a point of knowing just who make good, proper, well-mannered guests and who do not.

You careless girls and thoughtless men may

not know it; but these smiling, cordial hostesses, who welcome you with such warmth, have you all ticketed and mentally pigeonholed, and they know just what functions you will be invited to from the first of October to Ash Wednesday. They also know just which ones you will be left out of and to which the more attentive men will be invited.

What constitutes an attractive man? What value does a hostess put upon a well-bred guest?

First of all, it would do you no harm to stop and think for a few moments of your hostess. If you are fairly good-looking, well and good. It makes not the slightest difference with your invitations. The ugliest men I ever knew in all my life were the most attractive. Your hostess cares nothing for your looks. What has she invited you for? Put yourself in her place for a few moments and think.

It will do you good if you think first of all of the cost of entertaining. There are very few people in this world who can entertain with no thought of the expense. So you should, therefore, as an honest man, give your hostess the worth of her money. Remember, she is not a mere hotel-keeper, as a stranger might think from the manner in which her thoughtless guests treat her. She gives you all this pleasure, and it has cost her time and anxiety as well as money to bring all you young people together for, let us say, a house-party. I have known young men to be in a lady's home for a week and never speak to their hostess, except to ask for more, until the day of parting came, when they would take her hand, utter a few cut-and-dried remarks about what a good time she had given them, then dash down the steps to get the seat next to a certain girl, leaving the hostess quite positive that they would never give her another thought until her next invitation was issued.

Your hostess deserves some of your time and attention every day you are in her house. Yet when you are in a hotel you spend more time talking with the night-clerk than you devote to some of your hostesses. Pay your bill like a man! Don't sponge on her hospitality and go away in her debt, and leave her to the knowledge that you owe her something that you never will pay.

"Guest appearances" with one's hostess are a must.

If your hostess gives a dance you must ask her at least once. Even if she is purple-faced, fat, awkward and pop-eyed, it is a duty no gentleman can neglect. And if a married woman invites you to be the partner of a guest of hers, the first invitation of the evening belongs, not to the girl, but to the hostess.

I know men who actually grumble at being obliged to write notes of thanks afterward, sometimes for a two weeks' entertainment. They call them "bread-and-butter" letters, and frequently hostesses receive none at all from certain guests. What do you suppose these courteous, well-bred ladies think of such boorish manners?

Oh, do I hear a protest from all of you? "What? Am I expected to show specific attention during the winter to every married woman who entertained me during the summer?" Certainly you are!

You say you can't afford it? Then, in ordinary decency, don't put yourself under obligation by accepting invitations.

You say women make believe? We have to, in order to keep our society together. You claim that we smile on one and all alike. It is not true. If you were really popular with us you would know it. Your complaint of our artificiality is based on nothing less than the fact that we are polite to you when your selfishness and bad manners should really bar you from our doors forever. We are false, inasmuch as we don't have you kicked out of our drawing-rooms by the footman. You have eaten and drunk for years at our expense; have flirted with our prettiest, sweetest girls; yet have never paid one debt with so much as a "Thank you, ma'am."

It may be unjust, but whenever I see young people displaying flagrant selfishness; ignoring elderly persons; disregarding the known wishes of their hostess; rude to all except their own set, I always lay the whole blame upon the mothers.

Therefore, it is not a bad idea for a young man to bear in mind that his behavior in society advertises his mother. (1905) 🌶

Newfangled Fashion

An ACCENT ON à la mode

The Will-O'-The-Wisp

By J. W. FOLEY

Right here is Fashion, fickle dame, who no two years is quite the same; her parentage nobody knows; perhaps, like Topsy, she just grows; her other names are Vogue and Style, and she keeps busy all the while devising things so strange and queer, undoing what she did last year.

She's old as Time, yet always new; she's always busy, never through; she says "thumbs up" and up they go, and vice versa, as you know; your wife and my wife and the wives of all men chase her all their lives with breathless eagerness to see what styles are hers, and so do we; she darts by valley, hill and peak, capricious and with many a freak; what she may say or she may do, no matter—all the world does, too!

It is a merry chase she leads, and what the distance no one heeds; how she may travel, where may stir, the thing is to keep up with her; her moods are never twice the same, but we just grin and say we're game; next week she makes us throw away the kind of hats we buy to-day; today we rip and change and tear the things last week she bade us wear.

The hatters wait for her to speak before they trim another freak; and women watch her as the Sphinx to speak and say what quips and kinks shall be the rage; all her decrees are absolute; the bended knees of millions crook in homage meek and breathing's hushed that she may speak!

See women stout with diet slips and thin ones buying forms and hips; see waistlines moving up and down to make last week's to this week's gown; the switch that made puffs yesterday is braided now another way, and what was Himalaya's peak of hair is now a squatty freak; that bonnet we adore today tomorrow is a castaway.

A substantial head of hair was covered by a hat of equal proportions to create the properly feminine profile.

DRAWN BY KARL ANDERSON

And women dressed in style and vogue at noon find Fashion such a rogue, if they get home a little late their dresses are all out of date; the hat that was a dream at dawn may change the while you pin it on, and half an hour on the street may see a change of styles complete; for somewhere Fashion sits and smiles and ordains new and freakish styles, until no low, descending sun sees woman's wardrobe ever done! (1910) 🐛

The promenade provided opportunity for display of latest styles.

In fact, my whole philosophy of clothes, if such a shifting thing as dress has a philosophy, might be summed up in the one word Simplicity. I am sure that not all women will agree with me, and most men won't. The first thing I have in mind when I order a gown is its appropriateness for the occasion for which it is required. But frankly —and I don't think all women are frank about their clothes—I hate to see dresses, especially the shoulders, all fussed up with trimmings. The line from the seam on the shoulder to the bosom is the loveliest line in a woman and should not be broken. American women like to build out their shoulders, while French women try to make theirs look small. Nature intended women to have small shoulders and to be dainty rather than heroic. (1909) 🐛

Style and the Stage

By BILLIE BURKE

The fashion writers may say all they please about Paris setting the fashion for all things to wear feminine, but I don't think I am wrong when I say that fashion really radiates from the stage. At all the big "first nights" of modern plays in New York you can see fashionable dressmakers scattered through the audience. They are there mainly to get hints for costumes. They well know, if the play is a big success or the star is very popular, that it won't be many days before patrons will be coming in and saying: "I want a morning dress like the one Miss Blank wears in the first act of——"

Children's dress styles and lifestyles—a 1906 Kodak ad for Post.

The sleeves are so absurd;
They're tightly fitted at the top,
    And at the wrist they're shirred!
The shoulder-seams are far too long,
    The collars too high-necked;
I cannot wear my old gowns
    And keep my self-respect!   (1902) 🎵

Fashions for Gents

An EDITORIAL

For about a hundred years—since pants came in—there has been very little change in men's clothing. In this hundred years our railroads have been built, the commercial uses of electricity discovered, wealth and population have multiplied, the arts of peace have advanced. No doubt there is a connection between the two facts.

Every summer misguided friends of man try to organize a revolt against the coat. That hot, heavy and superfluous garment, they say, should be discarded in dog-days. The consensus, however, of masculine opinion repudiates them.

After thirty centuries of demoralizing experimentation the world has finally discovered the

Woman seems to have invented Fashion to hold in constant curiosity and eager mystery her loving painters and historiographers.

Regrets

By CAROLYN WELLS

I cannot wear the old gowns
    I wore a year ago,
The styles are so eccentric,
    And fashion changes so;
These bygone gowns are out of date
    (There must be nine or ten!)
I cannot wear the old gowns,
    Nor don those frocks again.

I cannot wear the old gowns,
    The skirts are far too tight
They do not flare correctly and
    The trimming isn't right.
The Spanish flounce is fagoted,
    The plaits are box, not knife;
I cannot wear the old gowns—
    I'd look like Noah's wife.

I cannot wear the old gowns,

Man seems to be totally ignorant of Fashion. The items in his wardrobe which go on with the least amount of thinking will no doubt comprise his favorite attire.

grand principle that it doesn't at all matter what men wear if it is always the same thing, so that they never have to think about it. Released from the distraction of picking out colors and flounces for our smallclothes and headgear we have harnessed the clouds and the waterfalls, cleared the wilderness, put down typhoid fever and learned to fly. Whoever seeks to set men thinking about clothes seeks to puncture the tire of progress. Any masculine garb is preferable to any possible change involving cogitation and debate. Men's costume may not be beautiful; but note what the world in pants has done, and stay an unseemly hand. (1910) 🍒

All's Fair in Fashion

An ABOUT-FACE

It may be permitted us to think that the day of wide eccentricity in dress has definitely passed, and that we enter with this twentieth century into a period of calm, or relative, wisdom, and, so to speak, into the adult age of fashion. Henceforward,

Fashion will evolve about one and the same aesthetic sentiment without return to the extravagance of our mothers. Our cosmopolitanism—this age of leveling commercialism, of uniform apparel, of travel, of utilitarianism—will always bring us back to a necessary simplicity—even in excessive luxury—and will prevent the makers and promoters of new styles from disregarding too brutally a dress appropriate to contemporary life. (1901) 🍒

The present epoch might fairly be called the Age of Buttons. It has been reckoned that the people of the U.S. unbutton 800,000,000 buttons every night when they go to bed, and rebutton the same number in the morning. Think how long it would take you to unbutton and button that number of buttons, and you will realize how important is the button in the scheme of our civilization. (1904) 🍒

How the Rich Young Girl is Given a High Finish

By MAY WARWICK

Finishing schools have come up since the American democratic ideal has begun to go down. Decades ago, when America assumed that she was still in the making, there were schools for girls, indeed, but the girls were never finished until their lives were finished.

But to-day, when family life and home training are in very rich homes an unknown quantity, when the home, indeed, is nothing but a huge hotel, about as conducive to companionship among its members as a hotel, and when the ideal is to escape from the community as not exclusive enough, the finishing school is selected to prepare the unlucky rich man's daughter for her future.

The great mass of finishing schools are attended by the daughers of the newly rich, by those who have money but have not yet social position. They have also a wrong kind of family life and false social ideals. No mother need send her daughter away to be trained if she is the right kind of mother, and, in ninety-nine cases out of a hundred, a good education can be given the girl in her home town or near by. But the mother is not seeking a good education. She is not thinking of preparing her daughter to be a rational human being, genuine and self-forgetful, but rather to take on social airs and graces, to make choice friends, to learn to climb industriously toward the upper heights, where she will one day (it is hoped) walk perfectly.

And the nature of the social education for which the girls are sent! They are to meet prominent people; sometimes an exclusive mother may be induced to come to an afternoon tea where the girls in the under strata look longingly at her and write home the news to their parents. Occasionally, a good-natured great man in politics or business will come (his wife and children in Europe); or a well-known author or musician will drop in for an hour to help glorify the school for a year.

In some schools almost a uniform is demanded, and while the students dress for dinner they must wear simple white gowns. Some schools even give girls lessons in the complete art of dressing, from shoelaces firmly tied to a collar firmly adjusted.

The difficulty is that the finishing-school girl

Unaffected and unpolished, this sweet young girl is about to undergo the rigors of becoming a young lady.

A successful student earns high marks in charm and poise.

merely self-assertive to simply shocking. She may be the type that smokes cigarettes and calls men by their surnames, or she may be merely a young empress who expects the world to bow to her and offers it in turn a self-satisfied face and a polished manner (except when unduly excited), who has never learned the old-fashioned definition of girlhood, self-effacement, gentleness and consideration for others. Her equipment is usually ability to chatter superficially about current topics and about people, a memory for who's who in America, and the power, perhaps, to conceive an elaborate entertainment; but she has no real information, no real resources, no real power to estimate the workings of the world outside her social environment, no skill to get beyond the conventional barriers that keep her in her place. The worst indictment against the system that has achieved her is that she is ignorant of anything that would fit her to be a proper wife or mother. She knows nothing useful." (1908) 🐾

does not wish to be inconspicuous, and if she takes on simplicity at all she does so as a pose which will make her conspicuous. She may learn indeed that she must not have a pompadour so large that she will be taken for a Fourteenth Street shopgirl. She may come down to breakfast so hastily dressed that she is reprimanded for having her collar on crooked, and yet she would prefer to go shopping in a gown that would make people turn to look at her.

Said a charming and cultivated woman who used to teach in a finishing school and who now teaches in a high school in a poor district of a big city: "I left my finishing school because I wanted some genuine material to work with.

"I may have to ask my little millgirls not to chew gum, but I can teach them something out of books, and they know what I mean when I talk to them of their duty to their neighbors and country. I do my little best to begin them, and their life will do the rest. I'd rather try my hand at this work, sordid surroundings and all, than at finishing the other type of girl or watching her when she is finished, which is worse.

"When she is finished she may be anything, from

The school has definitely furnished the finishing touches. But what about a fundamental education?

Shall I go to College?

By SENATOR ALBERT J. BEVERIDGE

Sundry thousands of young men and young women will soon be investing in frames wherein to display a bit of parchment, elaborately engraved with Latin words. But how about these degrees in course? What actual value have they? Who, except the possessors, ever think of them, unless to smile at them? And who would ever take at all seriously a young man or young woman who took his or her degree seriously? A man must speak for himself. A title of any kind is a farce. (1905)

When searching for my final answer to the question this moment being asked by so many young Americans, "Shall I go to college?" I answer in the affirmative. I do so admitting that a negative answer has been given by men whose opinions are entitled to the greatest possible respect. I admit, too, that nearly every city—yes, almost every town—contains conspicuous illustrations of men who learned how to "get there" by attending only the school of hard knocks.

A pause for intellectual communion between the sexes.

Mascot and master take a stand.

Remember, then—you who for any reason have not had those years of mental discipline called "a college education"—that this does not excuse you from doing great work in the world. Do not whine and declare that you could have done so much better if you had "only had the chance to go to college." You can be a success if you will, college or no college.

All you have to do in the latter case is to put on a little more steam. And remember that some of the world's sages of business have closed their life's wisdom with the deliberate opinion that a college education was a waste of time and an over-refinement of body and of mind.

Still, with all this in mind, my advice is this: Go to college. Go to the best possible college for *you*. Patiently hold on through the sternest discipline you can stand until the course is completed. It will not be fatal to your success if you do not go; but you will be better prepared to meet the world if you do go. I do not mean that your mind will be stored with much more knowledge that will be useful to you if you go through college than if you do not go through college. Probably the man who keeps at work at the business he is going to follow through life, during the years when other men are studying in college, acquires more information that will be "useful" to him in his practical career. But the college man who has not thrown away his college life comes from the training of his Alma Mater with a mind as highly disciplined as are the wrist and eye of the skilled swordsman; and as sharp as his sword.

Nobody contends that a college adds an ounce of brain power. But if college opportunities are not wasted, such mind as the student does have is developed up to the highest possible point of efficiency. The college man who has not scorned his work will understand any given situation a great deal quicker than his brother who, with equal ability, has not had the training of the university. A man who has been well instructed in boxing is more than a match for a stronger and braver man unskilled in what is called the "manly art." That is your college and non-college man over again with muscle substituted for brain.

The pennant for loyalty, the sweater for warmth.

If you go to college, young man, you have got to be in earnest, too. You have got to say to yourself: "I am going to make more out of what is in me than any man with like ability ever did before." You cannot dawdle—remember that. Imagine every day and every hour of every day that you are in the real world and in the real conflicts thereof instead of in college with its practice conflicts, and handle yourself precisely as you would if your whole career depended upon each task set for you.

Resolve to get absolutely everything there is to be had out of your college experience; and then *get it*. Get it, I say, for that is what you will have to do. Nobody is going to give it to you. The spirit with which you enter college is just as important as going to college at all. It is more important. For if a man has the spirit that will get for him all that a college education has to give he has the spirit that would make him triumph in a contest with the world even if he did not get his college education. It would only be a little harder for him: that is all.

There is one thing I must warn you against, however, the critical habit of mind which somehow or other a college education does seem to produce. This is especially true of the great universities of our East. Nobody admires those splendid institutions more than I do; but has not every one of us many times heard their graduates declare that an irreparable mischief had been done them while in those universities by the cultivation of a sneering attitude toward everybody—especially toward every other young man—whom they see doing anything actual, positive or constructive?

So I say to you: Believe in things. Believe in other young men. When you see other young men trying to do things in business, politics, art, the professions, believe in the honesty of their purpose and their ability to do well. Do not discourage them, do not sneer at them. That will only weaken yourself. Believe in other young men and you will soon find yourself believing in yourself. That is the most important thing of all: believe in yourself. (1905) 🦶

Yesterday, raw material. Today, a finished product. Tomorrow, the marketplace.

Confessions of a Letter Writer

By CHARLES BATTELL LOOMIS

My father had a good many ideas, and one of them was that the ability to write an elegant letter was an open sesame to the best that the world affords; and I agreed with father—then.

My father died when I was eighteen and I found that I must leave school and enter business at once. Not caring to be beholden to any of my father's friends, I studied the want columns of a New York paper at the East Westfield reading-rooms, and the very first day I saw something that seemed promising. I wanted to learn whatever business I entered from the ground up and I expected to begin as office boy, and so "Boy wanted to run errands and make himself generally useful. Must be neat. Apply by letter to H. Grant, P.O. Box 1447" struck me as being a good opening.

I was glad that Mr. Grant wanted the application to be made in writing, as I wrote a very ornate hand, full of flourishes, and was considered by my schoolfellows to be almost as good as that of old man Spencer himself. Also, for a boy of eighteen I was uncommonly well read, and I determined to show the man in need of a clerk that his needs and my qualifications dovetailed into each other.

There is a proverb to the effect that brevity is the soul of wit, but I did not intend to write a witty letter, so there was no need to be brief.

Mr. H. Grant:

Honored Sir: Although I have not the pleasure of your acquaintance, yet your advertisement in to-day's paper filled me with a desire to serve you in whatever capacity you may see fit. You ask for a boy and, although I am now entering upon man's estate, having just turned eighteen, I think that I can do a boy's work. I am a ready runner, and, should an affair cry haste, my speed would answer it. You will find me willing and prompt. As the greatest of all poets says:

The flighty purpose never is o'ertook.
Unless the deed go with it.

You will find my deeds go with your purposes.

You mention neatness as a requisite. My mother taught me that cleanliness was next to godliness, and if I had to take my choice of soup or soap I would choose the latter.

I hope to please you when I come to you, and who knows but that we may become great friends.

A generous friendship no cold medium knows,
Burns with one love, with one resentment glows.

Awaiting then your summons to join your caravan, as it were, and being filled with a spirit to serve you with all zeal, I am

Ransom Porson.

Twice rejected, but never deterred.

I did not get the job. But I did get a letter from Mr. Grant and I just happen to still have it.

Dear "Letter Writer": I wanted a plain, unadulterated office boy and not a polite letter writer. Apply for a position as correspondent in some seventeenth century house.
Yours in a hurry,
H. Grant.

Of course, I congratulated myself on having escaped service with so common a man and looked up the want column again. This time I found an advertisement that called for a nice-appearing boy to run errands and the address given was B.A. Smith, 71 John Street.

I was not above learning from experience, and this time I determined not to be so flowery, while yet giving a good idea of the sort of fellow I was. I spent half a morning on this letter, and when it was done I felt that it was a great pity that I could not step at once into a partnership instead of serving a more or less dull apprenticeship in clerkdom:

The eager job-hunter preys on the "want columns" daily.

Dear Mr. Smith: You want a boy. I want a place. You want him nice-appearing. Self flattery is odious, but I think I'll do.

Do you want him quick on his feet?
I have the feet.
Do you look for industry?
I am a bee.
Do you wish for intelligent service?
Hire Ransom Porson.

It is a singular thing that I always got answers to my remarkable letters, and Mr. Smith's was a treasure:

My dear Master Porson: Apply for a position with one of the comic weeklies—and you won't get it. Neither do I want you. You are too bright to be a mere office boy.

Yours, etc.,
B.A. Smith.

I was not cast down. I did not think my mania for writing letters was a curse, and I gayly sought the want column once more.

The advertisement that introduced me to a mer-

cantile life read:

Wanted a young man to act as correspondent in an office. Address M. Papadopulo, 136 Washington Street.

I did not know then what nationality Mr. Papadopulo represented, but I determined that this time I would please, and so I wrote:

Dear Sir: I have lost several chances at positions because when they asked for an errand boy I gave them an essay instead. You ask for a correspondent and I have half a mind to go to your office instead of writing, but as the carfare is an item I will instead give you a glimpse of my hand and style.

What is the nature of the correspondence that you want? I can quote you the poets or write in measured lines myself. Marry, give me the thoughts and I'll furnish the words.

Take me or leave me, you can't hurt my feelings. If this letter does not win me a position I'll write no more letters to you or for you.

Yours without a grain of hope,
Ransom Porson.

The next day I received a reply, ill-expressed and atrociously spelled, but full of joy to me:

Der Sur: You are god riter. I nead to hav you. Com an se me on to-moro morneng.

Yors truely,
M. Papadopulo.

I went that very day and found that Mr. Papadopulo was a Greek fruit merchant—a retail merchant. In fact his store was in the cellar and was not much bigger than a horse car. He wanted some one to keep his books, and thanks to my letter I got a position with him and *two dollars a week* at the very start, and he was such a nice little man that I stayed with him a year. (1903) ❧

True Conservation

By MAUDE RADFORD WARREN

The factory inspector is a relatively new force making for righteousness in these regenerating days of social reform. His is no easy position. He represents society, which is beginning to ask for a better kind of human being, objecting to men and women with anaemic bodies and dead souls, and still more objecting to having the power of children used up in shops and factories at a time when it ought to be going into brain and muscle.

The factory inspector, representing the thinking part of society, must, at considerable expense of spirit, see that greed and short-sightedness do not sap the strength of the wage-earners—children, women and men. His function is really not so much to inspect as to enforce the law.

If an inspector is visiting a doubtful factory, he may be received politely or gruffly, but what he is waiting for is the remark: "Just stay here a few moments; I'll have some one show you through."

That means a messenger is scurrying through the factory to hide away the children under fourteen and to close hatchways and clear obstructed passageways. In such a case the inspector does not wait to be shown through the factory, but pushes upon his way unescorted, leaving the manager to rely on the astuteness of the children themselves or the adroitness of the foreman.

Usually the manager contrives to maintain under all discoveries a fair degree of politeness toward the inspector, but there is one time when his manners fail him, and that is during a rush season when he is working his people overtime at night, and, counting on the inspector's hours of nine to five, does not expect interruption. But inspectors themselves can work overtime in a good cause, and around Christmas certain paper-box manufacturers are indeed fair game.

The manager—politely tolerant.

One gray-haired, handsome gentleman swore violently at a woman inspector who came late in the evening to his factory and questioned a tiny girl as to her age. The inspector was a beautiful creature with the air of expecting deference from men, but with nerves seasoned to certain kinds of brutality, and she persisted in her duty. The manager switched off the lights and she had to stumble in the dark till she could feel her way to the upstairs rooms where women were violating the ten-hour law.

The next day he sent word to the chief inspector that he did not mind inspection, welcomed it, in fact, but he wanted the person who was inspecting to be a lady and not a rude, interfering female.

The inspectors find less difficulty now than for-

The family troubles are heartrending, but so is the look of the ten-year-old child supporting it.

DRAWN BY EDWARD PENFIELD

merly in enforcing sanitation, although it is still not always easy to oblige proprietors to furnish ample and separate toilet facilities for each sex, and to provide a separate eating-room in factories where white lead, arsenic or other poisonous substances or gases are present under harmful conditions.

The inspector may not ask an adult any question about his wages, but he may so question a child and, indeed, may say anything to it that will bring out facts about its age, the amount of schooling it has had, and the number of hours it works. The child must show its age and school certificate and its employment ticket issued by the school authorities.

If the age certificate produced appears to have had the dates altered, the inspector calls her foreman. The child will weep and plead and at last tell the truth about her age. The foreman and the manager disclaim all responsibility.

"It's not our fault," they say. "We supposed the age certificate was all right. We haven't the time to go into those things. We'll discharge the child."

In a day or two a woman with a dirty shawl outlining her worn face will no doubt come to see the chief inspector, bringing the little girl. She'll beg for reinstatement and tell a pitiful story. Her husband is sick; she is sick; her elder son is a drunkard; the other son can't get work, and she depends on the wages of this child and her elder sister.

Admittedly a pitiful case, yet, on the other hand, the child under fourteen should not be burdened with the support of its elders. Frequently there is no real reason why it should not be in school; its parents simply look on it as a financial asset and want its earnings.

The community is beginning to understand not only the claim of the individual worker to reasonable, practical methods of safeguard from needless suffering, but also the claim that the profits of manufacture must not be bought at the expense of the life and health of citizens.

But it is one thing to have good laws and another thing to have them enforced. The difficulty is that labor laws may be enacted without any power whatever being supplied to carry them out.

Moreover, while the inspectors as a class are undoubtedly conscientious, they are not always thoroughly equipped for their work. If better salaries were paid better material could be had. More women should be appointed, not only because they will accept the inadequate salaries but because they are likely to be more permanent and can handle the children and women workers better than men inspectors can.

Last and always, what is needed is the continued and far-reaching education of the public. There is little use in having a good inspection department if it is not backed up by public opinion. (1910) 🌩

Outside, smokestacks emitted evidence of well-maintained equipment in sound working order. Inside, little thought was given to how the factory could save its most precious commodity—human machinery.

The Shadow of the City

By GROVER CLEVELAND

It must be abundantly apparent to all who have studied our beginnings as a Nation that its structure and its institutions were adjusted to the needs and aspirations of a virtuous, industrious and patriotic people—whatever might be the difference in their surroundings. It is not so apparent, however, that any especial consideration was given to the relations which should exist in the future of the Nation's development between its rural population and the larger communities which its trade and commerce might create. Generally speaking, it may be said of our pioneer settlers and of the makers of our Nation that their standards of life and their sympathies were most in accord with those who lived simply and whose occupations brought them near to the soil and scattered their habitations. Doubtless it was contemplated that cities would grow up, and that centres of trade and business would be established; but it may well be doubted if the minds of the fathers of the Republic compassed the expectation that in the future there would exist so many points of divergence between the populations of city and country as have actually supervened. It was utterly impossible to foresee a time when the growth of cities and the prevalence of their ambitions might threaten to overwhelm the wholesome sentiment which they loved to associate with rural life. It seems unprofitable to pursue our conjecture concerning their intentions further than to suppose that if these questions were considered at all, their solution was left to the good sense and wisdom of the succeeding generations.

So after several generations, we of the present day find ourselves confronted with a very serious problem concerning our urban and city life. How should these elements of our social and political existence affect one another? We know that each has its peculiar characteristics, and we believe that the mingling of these in proper proportions will assure our Nation's greatest strength and safety. In other words, we believe that the separate influences attaching to these modes of life should so supplement each other as to create a harmonious national development.

This, however, is predicated upon the theory that the influence and conditions of our city life are such as naturally grow out of its activities, unperverted and uncontaminated by baser motives; and that the conditions and influences of our rural life are of that sterling conscientious kind which keep alive a strong sense of public and private duty, and stimulate constant patriotism. (1903) 🍒

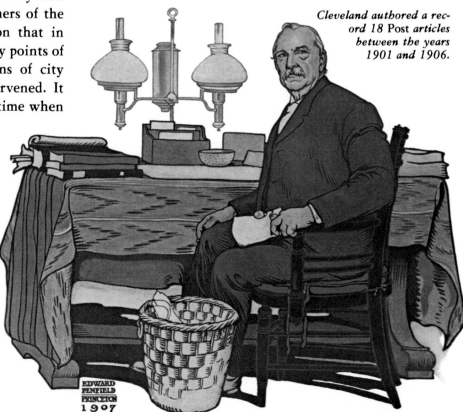

Cleveland authored a record 18 Post *articles between the years 1901 and 1906.*

Town and Country

An AIM TOWARD RECIPROCITY

"A crust eaten in peace is better than a banquet partaken in anxiety."—The Town Mouse and the Country Mouse *from* Aesop's Fables.

Growth of the Cities

An EDITORIAL

A quarter of a century ago the congestion of population in cities was the darkest cloud on the horizon of modern life.

Rapid transit and the telephone have changed the whole outlook. The growth of cities is no longer alarming, for the cities are growing in extent even faster than in population, and such overcrowding as remains is largely a mere traditional survival. City and country are merging, and it will soon be impossible to tell where one ends and the other begins.

A city used to be a little black dot on the map. Now it is a great splotch.

With the present facilities for transportation a man may readily live thirty miles from his business. And a thirty-mile radius, of course, is not the limit. It is only what a proper organization of the transportation business would put within our reach to-day without a single new invention. Rapid transit at a hundred miles an hour is plainly in sight, and that means cities of a hundred miles radius. It means the coalescence of New York, Philadelphia, Baltimore and Washington, or in other words, the complete obliteration of the line between city and country and between one city and another. Most of us may live to see the time when the terms "urban" and "rural" shall have become obsolete, and all life will be suburban. (1901)

Plain 'n Simple

By EDMUND VANCE COOKE

Country 'round is *rather* dull; town's a
  sort of match;
Landscape needed mendin', but the town's
  a blame poor patch.
"Ugly" is an ugly word, so I sha'n't call it
  such,
But just a look'll show that the town ain't
  very much.
Streets are only wagon-ruts, and sidewalks
  hit or miss,
Up a step for that one and down two jumps
  for this;
Just a string of straggly stores and houses
  sprawled about;
First thing every drummer asks is, "When's
  the next train *out?*"
"Cannon-ball" goes through here with a
  shudder at the sight;
Drops a mail-bag, maybe, as if pityin' our
  plight.
Last place you might ever call a pictcher or
  a po'm,
And yet some of us like the place; some of
  us call it home. (1901)

Medieval Methods for Modern Children

By MAUDE RADFORD WARREN

The thought of the Little Red Schoolhouse puts a welter of sentiment into the heart of the average American, whether he ever actually saw one or not.

Pictorially, it suggests little chubby children on hard benches, waiting their turn to go up and stand in line to spell, meanwhile surreptitiously munching apples or running to the waterpail in the corner. The source of a splendid grounding in the three "R's" was that Little Red Schoolhouse, and the magic gateway through which any boy could pass to the portals of the White House.

The descendant of the Little Red Schoolhouse is today a thing to marvel at. On one side of a crowded territory is a railroad; on the other side, a factory; in between is a red brick building, a high school four stories in height, with six entrances.

And through all this rigid, elaborate institution a mass, appallingly human, is trying to filter—the seething, uncalculated raw human product called boys and girls.

As it stands now, each child must get through each course in each grade so that the teacher in the grade above will realize that he has been well prepared. The child must have done a certain amount of work by the time he finishes the eighth grade, so that, in case he goes to high school, the teachers there will know that the grammar school has done its part well. This uniform course of study is deadening to both child and teacher.

Thus our public-school system, elaborate as it is, fails to meet the needs of all the people chiefly because the standards are academic, while what most students need are industrial and trade schools.

The little ones cluster in our schools, and the best and sincerest English they learn is the Salute to the Flag. To hear a roomful of children repeat those noble words would thrill even a heart discouraged over American politics. Surely the nation that can make those little descendants of hand workers love so well the flag that means to them opportunity and freedom has enough largeness and wisdom to evolve some day a system of education that will give the trusting young creatures a chance at the opportunity and freedom for which their fathers became a part of America. (1910)

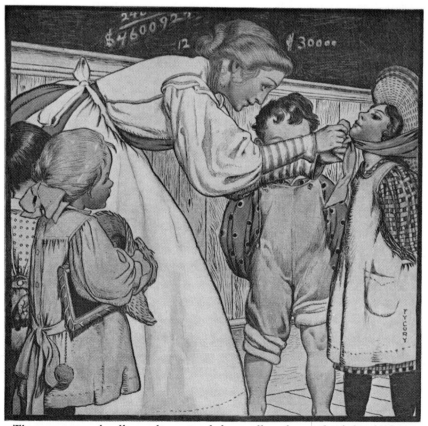

The one-room schoolhouse has expanded as well as the needs of the children.

An Appeal to the American Jokesmith

By BERT LESTON TAYLOR

That Americans are a humorous people has been denied, with show of truth. That we think we are a humorous people is no more to be denied than the jolly-good-fellowship of a certain Knight, whose Quest of the Silver Cup has entertained two nations.

It may properly be objected that true humor has little to do with much or most of what is labeled humor; this is a trail leading elsewhere. I have in mind the joke of commerce, the mainstay of the "comic paper," a popular term embracing all periodicals designed solely to amuse the public at large.

To the proposition that Americans are not a humorous people, but only think they are, perhaps no man will more readily assent than the editor of a "comic paper"; not so much because of the small number of good jokes in the market, as because of the enormous number of unsolicited and impossible contributions that stuff his daily mail.

Helpful hints come to him from all parts of the United States. Remuneration is usually fully expected, and quite frequently a staff position is also suggested.

A persisting type is the witty convalescent who, pending his return to the brickyard or rolling-mill, writes:

I don't make a business of writing jokes, but my friends tell me I really ought to be on a comic paper.

I think of a great many funny jokes. Here is one of them.

Which I omit.

Then there is the other unconscious comedian who informs the editor, in effect, that while he is waiting for the surgeon to come and saw his leg off he thinks he will jot down a few "funny things" to while the tedious hours away. "What do you pay for jokes?" he inquires. "What size paper should I use? and what kind of pen?" Which recalls the amateur jokesmith who once wrote to H.C. Bunner: "Editor Puck: What will you give me for the inclosed?" And Bunner's reply went: "Five yards start."

This query from a premature jokesmith in the Nutmeg State:

The editor's reaction to America's attempts at jokesmithing.

Dear Sir: Inclosed joke was received to-day—returned to me by you. I had taken your long delay in acknowledging its receipt as proof of its acceptance, and in consequence presumed too much by informing a literary friend that it would appear. I shall not be so rash next time. However, as you cannot publish it at an expense to yourself, I would respectfully ask if it may appear at my expense, and if so what will that expense be, minus, of course, the tell-tale marks of a paid contribution?

In 1896 the New York Journal *printed the first comics, featuring the antics of characters such as* The Captain and the Kids.

The foregoing specimens of amateur joking are drawn at random from several pigeonholes, and are contributed as a sidelight on the question: Are we indeed a humorous people? When we come to professional joke writing we reach a more melancholy survey.

Joke writing, as doubtless has been pointed out before, is profitable employ. The garden variety of joke fetches fifty cents. If it is good enough to warrant illustration it becomes a "comic," and fetches up to two dollars.

In contrast to the Connecticut gentleman's unhappy precipitancy is the cautious inquiry of a gentleman in Washington:

Gentlemen: I have a small joke I would like very much to send your firm. Would you kindly send me your instructions in doing the above said, and your terms also? It consists of about thirty words.

Americans readily appreciate a good joke. Creating one is another matter.

Prices being good, as the trade of writing goes, one supposes an army of professional jokesmiths. On the contrary, the successful purveyors of comicalities are few in number.

In the office of a comic paper a joke's a joke, although there's nothing in't. About once in six weeks the editor's grave features relax. His eyes have lighted on something like this:

WILLIE PEEBLES: The horse was goin'——
TEACHER: Don't forget your "g," Willie.
WILLIE: Gee, the horse was goin'——

Never before were jokes—good jokes—in such demand, and so hard to get, as now. Comic editors' safes are empty; staff writers pad the pages, because so little of the material that is contributed by the public is worth buying.

Any reader of this article who can turn good jokes can sell them. But one thing should be clearly understood at the outset: the expression is the thing. There are no new jokes, but there are still new ways of telling them. Individuality and a light wrist count for as much in jokesmithing as in the higher walks of literature. (1905) 🐛

Leisure

¶When a golf game and
a yacht race are technically
described in the same issue of a
newspaper the average reader finds
only partial comfort in the latest edition
of the unabridged dictionary, and the English
language has to seek introduction to the new members of its very mixed family. (1901)

The Good in Losing the Davis Cup

By CASPAR WHITNEY

While the loss of the Davis Cup, the second week in July, on the English Wimbledon courts, cannot honestly be claimed to have furnished a surprise, yet it certainly may be said to have given us material for thought, both as to the measure of our present playing skill and as to the foundation of our building for the future.

The Davis Cup is to lawn tennis what the America's Cup is to yachting. The record of the blue ribbon of the sea proves our efforts to have been directed by an intelligence which overlooked nothing essential in the make-ready, and produced, therefore, a champion fitted worthily and successfully to go forth as representative. The story of the blue ribbon of the courts hasn't so much of glory to shed upon America, but it is none the less interesting, and, indeed, has much of both entertainment and instruction to yield to research.

The cup was donated seven or eight years ago by Dwight F. Davis, of St. Louis, as an international challenge trophy to be played for annually, and the history of the matches for its possession is, to a large extent, the history of one of the most active periods of the game in America.

Competition for it also brings out the state of expertness in the game itself and shows as well what

Not bad form, considering the cumbersome attire.

Carol Aus

progress we have made in maintaining a state of preparedness—which, in fewer words, means keeping up the quality of the contestant—something that can be done only through healthful and open local competition, plenty of match-making and plenty of recruits.

American lawn tennis seems always to have a number of promising players who are heralded as "coming," but very few of our best men keep up their form after they have been graduated from college, or once they have entered upon their business careers. Just as they are beginning to mature—to reap the great benefits of experience—they quit.

The retired list of America cannot be duplicated in the lawn-tennis world in point of numbers and quality—and three-quarters of them are still young, most of them younger than the Australian who this year, after years of patient and persistent effort, succeeded in carrying off the highest honors that either America or England had to offer at Wimbledon.

The Americans were this year, and always have been, mere boys in comparison with their opponents; and I do not make this statement by way of excusing their defeat, but to commend the better sense of our rivals and to utter the wish that we might profit by their example.

In the thirty matches at singles and doubles which have decided the six contests for this cup, England has won sixteen, America eight by play and one by default, Australia three, and two in 1900 were never completed on account of rain after the American team had won the necessary three of the five scheduled.

America has won the trophy only twice within that period, in 1900 and 1902, and what appears to me to illustrate most significantly the kind of lawn-tennis progress we make is the fact that the Australians, whom the American players defeated three years ago, were the victors at last in 1907. That does not mean that the present form of the Australians is so much higher in 1907 than it was in 1905 (although it is some higher), but that *our* form is not so high.

However inadequately some of the essential interests of the game are served by its sponsors, there is no doubting the good which has been done the game by these Davis Cup contests; and the most good will come out of the defeats, and especially out of the defeat of this year, if the powers that be will not shut their eyes to what all of us who are friends of the game can see plainly.

But all this has

Great after the game, Coca-Cola was produced when Dr. John S. Pemberton in 1886 mixed 99% sugar and water and 1% "secret recipe." The "soft" drink (alcohol was "hard") caught on at the soda fountain, but wasn't bottled till 1899.

nothing to do with lawn tennis as a game for you and for me, and in that respect, at least, no criticism can be offered. It is not only a good game for us, but it is one of the very best to keep us in training if we are young and ambitious, or to keep us healthful and vigorous if we have reached that charitable time of "middle-aged."

And remember, if the middle-age period is passing in its inevitable turn, that you can still stay in the game with your boy by adding a foot to the height of the net, thus diminishing the killing pace without spoiling any of the fun.

It is very pleasing to note and to record the wide revival of general activity in this game. A few years ago the nets were rolled up and forgotten in the top attic; year before last the revival began, and this year the tennis court is as common on the lawn as the croquet wicket once was. (1907)

The Psychology of Baseball

By EMERSON HOUGH

There are different ways of telling when spring has come. You may, if you like, catch a burnished dove and examine it to see whether or not its iris has grown lovelier. You may guess it from the increased abundance of For Rent signs in adjacent flats. Your tailor announces it sometimes with a series of cards bearing the adjectives nobby, stylish, swell. Some depend upon the appearance of the robins which have come to nest again, whereas others rely upon the second column of the editorial page, and yet others most depend upon the appearance of the old woman who sells sassafras bark at the corner of the office building on Main Street.

A yet surer way is to examine the morning paper. When it begins to abound in half-page pictures of a badly bent gentleman, standing with one foot in the air and with one hand encased in a pillow, you may be sure that spring is either here or hereabout. The art of newspaper portraiture has advanced very swiftly of recent years, so that in eight cases out of ten a careful observer can tell the difference between the pictures of Philander C. Knox and Mike Donlin, of President Taft and Muggsy McGraw. The last-mentioned celebrity in each case is apt to have more space on the page. When these pictures of contorted gentlemen with initials on their bosoms begin to average from ten to thirty to the double-page, then you may have almost mathematical assurance that spring, and consequently baseball, is with us once more.

Of course, every healthy boy has during his youth played baseball or its equivalent, and, in order to escape the alternative of learning to play the piano, I played ball as a boy; but I am obliged to state, admit or confess that I have never in my life seen a game of professional baseball, and had always purposed never so to do; because by so doing not only would I extinguish my sole existing claim to any sort of distinction, but would remove from the field of possibility the only living American in position to write calmly as well as impartially regarding the singular phenomena of our national pastime.

The brave gentleman who stands directly in the line of fire, who dons face mask and chest protector and keeps his receiving hand in a "pillow"—that's the team catcher.

The other morning, when I stepped on the Elevated train the guard smiled at me with unusual warmth as he stepped on my foot and tried to squeeze me with the gate. "Rather bad weather for dem Cubs, eh?" he remarked. "But I guess it's warmer down to de Hot Springs."

No, I do not know who or what the Cubs are, or why they should be at the Hot Springs, but I made some knowing comment to the guard, and finished the morning journey in comfort. At the foot of the stairway downtown I paused to buy a paper. "Here y'are, sir," said the newsboy. "It's about de fight between Ban Johnson an' dat bloke Moify."

I have no just conception of the identity of Mr. Ban Johnson, and I do not know that bloke Moify at all, but naturally the remark of the small newsboy caused some curiosity.

To one unskilled—that is to say, to the only one unskilled—in the technical features of this great American sport, it is difficult to understand what baseball is about, but it may with a certain amount of confidence be asserted that it probably is about something. Again, anyone who has read Kant's *Critique*

The ever-popular slide—a sideline of the sport supposedly invented by Abner Doubleday. Actually, baseball was more an adaptation of other games than an original invention.

ANTON FISCHER

A pair of true baseball lovers, eager to polish their game? Or a couple of truant piano students? Only their mothers know for sure.

of *Pure Reason* can figure out that baseball is not the sole occupation of the American people, because a certain amount of other business seems to be transacted during the year. Business is attended to more especially during the winter months, before the days when the sport, pastime, mania, madness or hysteria has attained its full virulence.

It is now generally understood that baseball fever is carried by mosquitoes, but science has thus far discovered no serum or other corrective instrumentality which gives any medical control over the malady. It is far more deadly than the sleeping sickness, because the latter in time will run its course, whereas the baseball germ, lying dormant during the winter, renews and increases its activity cumulatively from year to year; and, although it seems not definitely to shorten the life of the victim, produces in him eccentricities and hallucinations such as to unfit him for lucid conduct or the transaction of the ordinary business of life. Moreover, the disease is communicable and highly contagious. I firmly believe that I owe my own immunity to my invariable practice of sleeping under a net, summer and winter. (1909)

A Football Fable

By REGINALD WRIGHT KAUFFMAN

It was an autumn evening,
   Three-Thousand-Five A.D.,
And old Professor Jay Ethnol
   Was strolling back from tea,
And by him sported on the pave
His five-year winsome grandchild
   Dave.

They saw before them suddenly
   A curious old mound,
Half like a knot of sculptured men
   A-twisting on the ground:
The lad in piping treble flat
Asked: "Holy smoke, Grandpop,
   what's that?"

Old Ethnol looked it o'er and sighed:
   "Alas, alas!" said he,
"Those are the fellows brave who once
   Won a great victory.
I guess they got so badly mixed
They never could get free."

"Now tell me what they scrapped about!"
   Inquired the eager Dave;
"Or did they fight for native land,
   Or did they free the slave?"
The old man shook his head of snow:
"None but the Rules Committee know.

"But 'twas the Bulldogs,"
      he pursued,
   "Who tanned the
         Tiger's hide;
Although the reason for it all
   I never could decide;
But all the girls declared," said he,
"That 'twas a famous victory.

"With unintelligible yells
   The air split open wide,
And many a mother cheered to see
   How well her brave boy died."
"That seems," said Dave, "a rotten shame."—
" 'Twas necessary to the game.

"They say it was a splendid sight
   When the last yard was won:
Helmets and nose-guards, splints and stays,
   Shone bloody in the sun,
And forty ambulances wheeled
The happy victors from the field.

"And everybody praised the Coach
   Who taught them body-blows."—
"But what good came of it at last?"—
   "Why, all the wide world knows
It killed or cured," was Jay's retort:
"Ah, 'twas a mighty manly sport!" (1906)

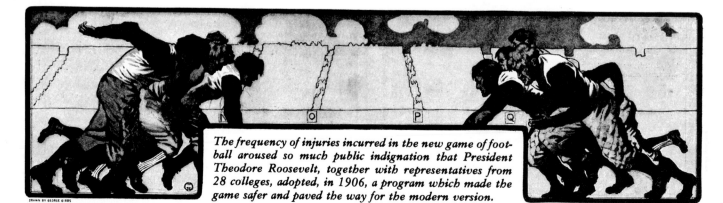

The frequency of injuries incurred in the new game of football aroused so much public indignation that President Theodore Roosevelt, together with representatives from 28 colleges, adopted, in 1906, a program which made the game safer and paved the way for the modern version.

DRAWN BY GEORGE GIBBS

Vaudeville and Vaudevillains

By PERCY G. WILLIAMS

In 1900, Percy G. Williams erected the Orpheum Theater in Brooklyn, New York; by the time he wrote the following article (1909), he owned and operated a total of eight theaters in and around the city of New York.

Scarcely ten years ago a trip to a vaudeville theater was regarded as a sort of slumming expedition; today no town is complete without a vaudeville house, and nearly everybody at some time attends a performance there. It has not only become our most popular form of amusement, but is attended each year by more people than any other kind of public diversion. The vaudeville theater is the people's playhouse. The reasons for this are that, first, it appeals to a great variety of tastes; and, second, the prices are reasonable.

While the story of vaudeville, as we now know it, is not so long and involved as the story of the legitimate dramas, it has, nevertheless, experienced a rather interesting development.

Vaudeville really goes back into the centuries. Originally *Vaux-de-Vire*, it was the name given by Basselin, a French poet of the fifteenth century, to his convivial songs first sung in the Valley of the Vire. Subsequently vaudeville came to be any short comic piece with song, pantomime or dance. In

modern French poetry a vaudeville is a light, gay song, embodying satire or burlesque, sung by the common people to a popular air.

The forerunner of the present-day vaudeville performer, however, was the old-time minstrel who amused our fathers before and after the Civil War. Then came the concert-hall artist, who later appeared in what was known as the variety house. This got its name from the fact that it afforded a variety of entertainment, mostly singing, dancing and fun-making. These houses appeared during the opera-bouffe days when tights were necessary adjuncts of every musical show. It followed that the variety shows included many persons in tights. Those shows were something like the burlesque companies of today in which there are hefty Amazons carrying spears.

I got started in the amusement business back in the seventies as a boy with Colonel William E. Sinn, a well-known variety theater manager in Baltimore. In the nineties I had two variety theaters and a summer resort.

I believed that two performances a day would be better in vaudeville than the continuous show, so in 1900, acting on this theory, I formed a company

that built the Orpheum Theater in Brooklyn, and began the "two-a-day" shows now generally given in vaudeville theaters. I permitted smoking in one balcony and called it a "smoking balcony," which is today a feature of many vaudeville houses.

Most vaudeville managers then believed that one "headliner" was enough to carry a bill. I felt that every act should be a good one. The old bills had involved a weekly payroll of from $1000 to $1500. My first bill at the Orpheum cost $3000. My friends in the business thought I was headed for ruin. They called it the era of frenzied vaudeville. But the people seemed willing to pay for it. I began to import European novelties, stars like Albert Chevalier, Alice Lloyd and Vesta Victoria.

In vaudeville you must always get fresh audiences, because with them you win regular patrons. For example, if I advertise Vesta Tilley I am bound to get to my houses people who do not ordinarily go to vaudeville, but who want to see a big star. Then they sit through the rest of the bill; they may like the house. Later, if they have nothing definite to do, they will go to a vaudeville show. It's like showing a good sample.

After building the Orpheum I invaded New York, with the result that, at the present time, I have eight vaudeville houses in the greater city. In the development of these theaters I had one object in mind, and this object, I think, is peculiar to vaudeville. To understand it, it must be borne in mind that a vaudeville feature cannot have a run like a play. You must change your bill constantly if you want to keep your clientèle. Therefore my plan was to build theaters in various localities and draw each week on the people of that section. I call my

theaters neighborhood theaters. There are many of them in London. I have a theater in the Bronx, Harlem, the upper West Side, two in Brooklyn, in East New York and at Greenpoint. I can keep an act going for seven or eight weeks on my own personal circuit. I arrange the bills so that each one has a particular appeal for the people of the locality in

What began as a pantomime to offset the Comédie-Française evolved into a light musical drama of spoken dialogue interspersed with songs.

which it is played. Harlem wants more laughs than the upper West Side of New York, and so on.

My own belief is that vaudeville has just begun to come into its own. It is destined to a development that will almost put the legitimate playhouse in the background. I have been asked many times if I thought the moving-picture show—the canned drama—would drive out or hurt the vaudeville business. It has helped rather than hurt.

As vaudeville has developed, so has the cost of operation greatly increased. In addition to a headliner, who must be a star, there must also be at least two features which may be headliners elsewhere. One of the rules in vaudeville, however, is, "Once a headliner not always a headliner." A successful bill today must have ten and, possibly, twelve acts. In many houses moving pictures are always given.

The moral side of the bill has improved, too. Repulsive acts have been cut out; feats that shock the audience are barred; even the man who does a tramp act must wear a clean-pressed shirt, despite the fact that it is contrary to the ethics of the hobo.

The old-time weekly payroll for artists has grown from $1000 to $7000. Yet the value of these high-priced bills is not always appreciated, as an episode which I now recall shows. To celebrate the fifth anniversary of the opening of the Orpheum I put on what was probably the most expensive vaudeville offered up to that time. It cost $9000 for the week. I got the best acts from every country and called it The International Topliners' Tournament. A week later I met a prominent Brooklyn business man on the street. He said to me:

"I went to your theater last week. Fine building."

"How did you like the bill?" I asked.

"Well, those were great moving pictures you had," was his reply. My $9000 all-star cast had been wasted on him.

This brings me naturally to the subject of the vaudeville audience. Just as the vaudeville field and its people form a separate and distinct amusement world, so is the vaudeville audience peculiar to itself. The regular vaudeville-goer is a keen and discriminating judge. What he wants, summed up, is the greatest amount of diversified entertainment with the least possible pathos. "Cut out the heartaches," he says, "and give us a song and dance." He wants to be amused, not grieved; he goes to bury sorrow, not to praise it. Above all, he wants the optimistic, not the uplifting spirit. He has a fine scorn for the so-called "high-brow" act; he wants no literature on his stage; he desires his entertainment straight and unadulterated.

At first aimed toward a masculine audience, by the 1890's vaudeville was considered family entertainment. Magicians, acrobats, jugglers, singers and dancers—it took a number of new acts to turn the head of the truly discerning vaudeville-goer.

All vaudeville bills are changed each week; hence the Monday afternoon audience is the critical one. Most of the regulars go then. They follow the various acts as a follower of the race-track watches past performances. They can tell you the form of every feature. Most of them have their list of favorites.

The vaudeville gallery god is as keen as his brother who fills the roost of the other theater. His is the real verdict. He knows when the heart-throb has the real thrill and when it is forced; and he is quick to express his judgment.

Laughs are the barometers of vaudeville acts. Sometimes when a turn is put on for the first time people are stationed out in the audience to count the laughs. It takes a good act to make a record of "a laugh a minute." (1909) 🌀

The Nickelodeon

By JOSEPH MEDILL PATTERSON

The first motion-picture theatre, or "nickelodeon," was opened in Pittsburgh, Pa., in Nov., 1905. Up until that time, the motion-picture had been merely an incident of vaudeville.

Three years ago there was not a nickelodeon, or five-cent theatre devoted to moving-picture shows, in America. To-day there are between four and five thousand running and solvent, and the number is still increasing rapidly. This is the boom time in the moving-picture business. Everybody is making money.

The nickelodeon is tapping an entirely new stratum of people, is developing into theatregoers a section of population that formerly knew and cared little about the drama as a fact in life.

The drama of conflict.

The character of the attendance varies with the locality, but, whatever the locality, children make up about thirty-three per cent of the crowds. For some reason, young women from sixteen to thirty years old are rarely in evidence, but many middle-aged and old women are steady patrons, who never, when a new film is about to be shown, miss the opening night.

The most popular films run from fifteen to twenty minutes and are from five hundred to eight hundred feet long. One studio manager

Affordable to many.

said: "The people want a story—a story with plenty of action. More story, larger story, better story with plenty of action—that is our tendency." Most of the shows have musical accompaniments. The enterprising manager usually engages a human pianist with instructions to play "Eliza-crossing-the-ice" when the scene is shuddery, and fast ragtime in a comic kid chase. Where there is little competition, however, the manager merely presses the button and starts the automatic going, which is as apt as not to bellow out, "I'd Rather Two-Step Than Waltz, Bill," just as the angel rises from the brave little hero-cripple's corpse.

The moving pictures were used as chasers in vaudeville houses for several years before the advent of the nickelodeon. The cinemetograph or vitagraph or biograph or Kineto-

One nickel got you fifteen minutes of viewing pleasure, so long as you didn't spit, swear, smoke or let the baby cry.

scope (there are seventy-odd names for the same machine) was invented in 1888-1889. Mr. Edison is said to have contributed most toward it, though several other inventors claim part of the credit.

The first very successful pictures were those of the Corbett-Fitzsimmons fight at Carson City, Nevada, in 1897. The Jeffries-Sharkey fight of twenty-five rounds at Coney Island, in November, 1889, was another popular success.

Within the past year an automatic process to color films has been discovered by a French firm. The pigments are applied by means of a four-color machine stencil. Beyond this bare fact, the process remains a secret of the inventors.

Those "interested in the poor" are wondering if the five-cent theatre is a good influence, and asking themselves gravely whether it should be encouraged or checked (with the help of the police).

Is the theatre a "good" or a "bad" influence? The adjectives don't fit the case. Neither do they fit the case of the nickelodeon, which is merely the theatre democratized.

Whether for weal or woe, humanity has ceaselessly striven to complicate life, to diversify and make subtle the emotions, to create and gratify the new and artificial spiritual wants, to know more and feel more both of good and evil, to attain a greater degree of self-consciousness; just as the one fundamental instinct of the youth, which most systems of education have been vainly organized to eradicate, is to find out what the man knows.

In this eternal struggle for more self-consciousness, the moving-picture machine, uncouth instrument though it be, has enlisted itself on especial behalf of the least enlightened, those who are below the reach even of the yellow journals. For although in the prosperous vaudeville houses the machine is but a toy, a "chaser," in the nickelodeons it is the central, absorbing fact, which strengthens, widens, vivifies subjective life; which teaches living other than living through the senses alone. Already, perhaps, touching him at the psychological moment, it has awakened to his first, groping, necessary discontent the spirit of an artist of the future, who otherwise would have remained mute and motionless.

The nickelodeons are merely an extension course in civilization, teaching both its "badness" and its "goodness." They have come in obedience to the law of supply and demand; and they will stay as long as the slums stay, for in the slums they are the fittest and must survive. (1907) 🐚

Mystery and intrigue.

Drama by the Foot

By VALENTINE KARLYN

The day when we were pleasantly surprised by the kinetoscopic presentation of such ordinary events as the arrival and departure of railway trains or the coming and going of the crowds on the boardwalk of Atlantic City is over. Making a moving picture now involves more or less creative effort and innovation.

It is questionable if the theatrical managers of the world have ever so carefully

The power of realism.

felt the pulse of the great public as have the men who make moving pictures. The multitude undeniably gets what it wants. It likes melodrama and farce, and accordingly there is no end of film plays in which the villains are foiled by beautiful heroines and handsome heroes, and in which awkward men make themselves ridiculous. Variety is the spice of the moving-picture show. Change, change and change again is what the moving-picture groundlings crave. They get it as they can never get it in the most kaleidoscopic melodrama, the tawdriest novel, or the yellowest of yellow journals.

Current events are often drawn upon to furnish the subjects of the most popular films.

To reproduce the famous storming of San Juan Hill a battle was fought in the Orange Mountains. *The Great Train Robbery*, a film that

Heroine or victim?

cost $20,000, was taken in part near Paterson, New Jersey, with the assistance of a specially-engaged train and a company of one hundred men and women to act as passengers, train-crew and bandits. One filmmaker conceived the idea of reproducing Custer's last fight, and to that end he brought a band of Sioux Indians from the West, among whom were three chiefs who had actually participated in the tragedy that cost Custer and 300 of his men their lives. Such is the stuff popular films are made of.

The stage manager reigns supreme. His slightest mandate, usually colored with picturesque, impatient epithets, is obeyed as if he were a captain drilling a company of soldiers. Often the actors know nothing of the plot. The stage manager rehearses the play scene by scene, ten or a dozen times. When the characters are sufficiently drilled he gives the word, "Ready for the picture," and the players perform their parts as the camera shutter clicks. The camera operator rarely has an opportunity of turning the crank for any length of time, so exacting, rigorous and pedantically fussy is the stage manager. Scenes are repeated over and over again, and yards of film are destroyed before he is satisfied. A hundred feet of film may represent a morning's hard work and perhaps a whole day's work.

Curiously enough, the actors and actresses must talk, for sound is apparently necessary to express human emotions. The villain in a photographic melodrama cannot help hissing "Cur-r-rse you!" into the shrinking heroine's ear, nor can the hero refrain from shouting "By Heaven, I *will* save her!" although the millions that will see him on the screen will never thrill at the words. (1909)

Autobiography of a Clown

By JULES TURNOUR

Jules Turnour was a lead clown for the Ringling Brothers show from 1886 to 1929. He died in 1931.

I suppose it was destiny that I should be a clown, because I was born in a circus wagon. My mother always told me that the first thing I saw when I looked out was Albro, the old French clown, who sat in the sun, whitening his face. More than once my baby cries mingled with the jests he hurled at the audience. I was, in truth, a child of the circus.

When I was six years old my father took me to London. On the way there he told me that the time had come when I should begin my life's work. When you are born in the circus you must follow the unwritten rule of the circus, which is that you must stay with the circus. The result was that I was apprenticed to the Conrads, who were a famous acrobatic "family."

Every great group of acrobats that you see in the circus, no matter if they do a trapeze act, tumble, ride bicycles or bareback, is called a "family." Now the interesting thing is that they are not real families at all. They develop into groups simply because they take in apprentices, train, develop and make them part of their troupes.

It was decided that I should be a contortionist. To be one, you had to be "a close bender"—that is, bend so close that the two extremes of your body meet. While you may have been born supple, it takes lots of hard training to be a good contortionist. By the time I was eight years of age I was regarded as a good contortionist. I was sixteen when my slavery days ended and I was free to go. After a year of

freedom I became ill. One day I almost collapsed during my act. I went to a hospital and the doctor told me I could not work for years. Upon hearing this, the ringster said to me:

Jules, you are a good mimic. Why don't you try clowning?

I thought it was a good idea. I had always been interested in the clowns of the shows; as an apprentice I would often steal off after training and watch them practicing.

The clowns of those days were "talking clowns." They talked as they worked. The circuses were much smaller then, and it was not hard to get the interest of the people. The clown had to be a good

The question is not When *will these two start to perform?* but *Which* un-*predictable character will break into antics first?*

acrobat and a clever comedian. He had to be a good pantomimist, too. This enabled him to get engagements on the variety stages during the winter months when work at the circus was slow.

When people ask me what underlies the business of clowning I always say, "Mimicry." That is the first requirement. Good clowns are good pantomime artists. We must first see ourselves as others see us.

As I came to study clowning I found that it was difficult work. When you see a clown make a funny fall it looks very easy and natural. But it is done only after long, hard practice. You have to study every step of that fall. Unless the funny fall is natural it fails utterly. The tall, peaked, clown hat

Barnum & Bailey rivaled Ringling Bros. until the 1919 merger.

was a great aid to the clown then. It was used a great deal more than now. The clown would come out with seven of these hats, one piled on the other. Then he would toss them up in the air and catch them on his head, or he would whirl them on to the head of another clown. Usually, only the large circuses ever carried more than one clown.

One of the most successful clown tricks of those days was known as the Peter Jenkins act, so named because a clown named Peter Jenkins first did it. The ringmaster and the clown came into the ring and the former made the announcement that Mademoiselle La Blanche, or any other high-sounding name, "the world's greatest equestrienne," would do her sensational act "as performed before all the crowned heads of Europe." Then a magnificent horse would be brought in. After the horse had pranced around the ring a commotion was heard in the "pad-room," the tent where the trappings are put on the circus stock for the rings. It is just outside the main tent. Then an attendant came rushing in and whispered something to the ringmaster. He seemed much shocked and then announced:

"I am very sorry, ladies and gentlemen, to be obliged to announce that Mademoiselle La Blanche has been kicked by a horse and is unable to appear," whereupon the clown pretended to shed tears, drawing in the audience.

In a moment a man who was very seedily dressed arose from among the spectators. He seemed to be under the influence of liquor, for he shouted:

"This show is a fake. I came here to see that lady ride and I won't be humbugged." With that he started for the ring. Of course, the whole show halted; everybody was keenly interested, for they thought it was the real thing.

Approaching the ringmaster the man again upbraided him. Then the ringmaster said:

At the circus, the spirit of wonderment abounds in light of the fantastic. Here, an unlikely trio performs an uncommon spectacle.

DRAWN BY
J. C. LEYENDECKER

"You seem to be so smart, I suppose *you* think you can ride."

"You bet I can," was the reply. He started toward the horse.

"I warn you," continued the ringmaster, "you will get hurt." But the man ignored the warning and took off his coat. Then he laboriously climbed on the back of the horse, while the interest of the crowd became intense. Nearly every person who goes to a circus expects to see some one hurt.

At any rate, the drunken man finally got on the horse, pulled a bottle from his pocket, took a farewell swig and then proceeded to take off more of his clothes. Meanwhile, the horse had started. As the animal walked around the ring the man's clothes fell to the ground. In a moment he stood revealed, clad in tights and spangles, while the horse, feeling his master on his back, began to gallop. Then the crowd saw that it had been fooled by a clever trick. It took a first-class clown to do this act, because he had to be a good actor and rider.

The clown's work also involves much thought and mental preparation. He has to be constantly putting new wrinkles into his

A delicate balancing act.

The sure circus sensation.

work. Every act that he does is carefully studied out and rehearsed. I have practiced a fall for a month. You may have noticed that clowns act in pairs or trios. This is due to the fact that every clown act, no matter how ludicrous or how simple, must tell a story. It is really a small drama or comedy. If the clowns, for example, wear soldiers' uniforms, they give an idea of a camp, a battlefield or some definite picture. Like everything else the clowning must be timely. The clown plays on a vogue. It may be Salome, or The Merry Widow, or the peach-basket hat, or the sheath gown. He must make his act a perfect piece of mimicry. Next, he must first look funny and then act funny. It is not always easy.

But when you are once a circus clown you are always a circus clown. Many die with the show. The white that we put on our faces is like the grease-paint the actors use. It never comes off. This is the traditional clown face. Both the costume and the face of the clown have undergone little change in a hundred years. It is, perhaps, the only amusement act that has kept its integrity all these years. Take the slapstick, the bladder and the funny fall and you have the original clown's stock in trade. It remains today. Unless I am mistaken it will remain for another hundred years. (1909) 🦐

The Profits from Laughter

By FREDERIC THOMPSON

Frederic Thompson owned and operated Luna Park, one of several parks which comprised Coney Island at that time. His park sported over 30 shows and rides, all of his own creation.

The fundamental something in Scenic Railways, Bump-the-Bumps, the Tickler, the Virginia Reel, the Chutes and a score of other well-known park amusements which in their incubator days were children's games, coupled with the community spirit which they raise as a whole carload of us—friends, strangers, men, women, young and old—whirl up and down and around, makes these rides perennially successful. We laugh hysterically, we clutch the sleeves of strangers as we dash down to some dizzy depth, we jostle one another good-naturedly and we scream with laughter when an old gentleman's hat blows off, until finally, at the bottom, when we leave the car, our sides are tired from laughing and our hearts are at peace with all the world. Our enjoyment has come from the people around us more than from the ride. We have made our own show and, like children, have given audible signs of having appreciated it. The laughter engendered by any ride, show or other amusement device is a prime factor in the success of any and every summer park and exposition. It is the second of the two absolute rules of my business. If you allow your public to aid in the work of amusing themselves, and make them laugh while they are doing it, you are on the highroad toward success and dividends. In the serious business of amusing a flannel-garbed, straw-hatted, midsummer populace everything between a simper and guffaw means money in the bank. Laughter comes from good nature, and good nature is the outcome of the carnival spirit, without which no exposition and no amusement park can hope to succeed.

My Luna Park on Coney Island is nothing more than a grown-up toyshop. In it men and women take the place of tin automatons. That is why it is successful. In the future I shall not try to invent new and extravagant amusements; I shall aim to be an adapter, and the things I shall adapt are the simple toys which have the approval of healthy-minded, pleasure-loving little boys and girls. After a considerable experience in providing entertainment for America I have reached the conclusion that people do not change, nor do amusements; they only grow. Men and women are nothing more than children grown tall, and the Shoot the Chutes is an adult cellar-door down which you and I used to slide in the golden days when play was everything; when responsibility had never been dreamed of; when Santa Claus was a principal god and when we decided from personal experience what games we liked best. I have found in a toyshop the models for a world's amusement exposition.

I am speaking from an experience probably greater than that of any other American showman, because it includes every angle of the vast amusement field, and never have I built an unsuccessful elaboration of a toy or child's game. This statement does not carry with it the assumption that the elaboration is successful because in microcosm it was a delight in the days of knickerbockers and knee-length gingham dresses. For a proper understanding of my argument you must believe me when I say again that grown-ups are nothing more than elongated youngsters; that Directoire gowns are direct descendants of calico slips; that likes, amusements, brains, languages, people do not change—they only grow. In Luna Park I allow no performance to run more than twenty minutes, for the excellent reason that I know it would fail if it did. That is why all summer attractions must be speedy, dramatic, to the point and simple.

Showmen have come to realize that people like to laugh, that their bank accounts are proportionate to their ability to make grown-ups feel like youngsters, that they must develop a carnival spirit to keep out of bankruptcy, and that the days of quiet, pictorial entertainment have gone forever. And, it would seem that the more ridiculous the

Almost *as good as being there, peeks are free—and not allowed.*

Sophistication veils the daring of adolescence, target of the amusement ride.

amusement the greater is its popularity. Rides are so popular that there can be no doubt they have come to stay. They are a natural result of the American love of speed. Just as we prefer the fastest trains, the most powerful motor-cars, the speediest steamships and the fastest horses, so we like best the amusement rides which furnish the biggest thrill. Take two rides—one a quiet, picturesque, comfortable trip, in which everything is serene, and the other a neck-breaking dash uphill, around curves and down perpendicular declines—and the crowd will pick the supposedly dangerous one every time. Nothing is too hazardous for a midsummer throng filled with the carnival spirit.

Have you ever stopped to think how much thought, how many men, how much ability and how much money are required to make midsummer America laugh? The investment in Luna Park alone is two million six hundred thousand dollars, and for four months in the year twelve hundred persons are on the payroll. It is a serious business—making a nation laugh.

Yet, if a man who has been grinding all the week can, by a visit to some midsummer enclosure of fun, learn to laugh, he has learned how to go back to his home, where everything should be happy and bright; he has learned how to go back to his work next day; he has learned to take heart.

That is the value of a laugh. (1909)

The County Fair

By HOLMAN F. DAY

Is he judge or contestant?

There is just one bright morning in the fall when "pap's" stentorian "Rout out now, boys; time for the chores!" brings the youth of the household out of bed "all standin'. "

That is the opening morning of the Cattle Show and Fair down at the Corners. It makes no difference what Corners. There is not a county in all New England so far behind in commerce and enterprise that it doesn't have its own fair.

A crisp morning, the rising sun quivering in mellow warmth through the yellowing maples on the eastern hillside, savory scents from the ripeness of autumn's gardens just over the old stone walls, the girls on the back seat of the bench wagon, "dad" and "marm" on the front seat, little son on a cricket between their knees, plenty of hard-boiled eggs, apple pie, tarts, plum cake and pickles in a big basket under the seat—these are the elements of an auspicious start for the day of the annual fairing.

There is never a moment of the whole fair that is "more titrivating" to mother, the girls and son than while the team is halted at the gate so that "pap" can buy the tickets at the little hole in the fence.

Mother and the girls and son are precious glad when father has completed his negotiations at the ticket window, exchanged greeting and handshakes with two or three rugged agriculturalists who are standing around the gate with whips in their hands waiting for the hired men to arrive with the stock, and has counted his change twice to be sure that it is all there.

"Come, father, do hurry up," says one of the girls. "We are missin' the whole show."

"Hain't nothin' special goin' on at eight o'clock in the mornin'," grunts "pap" as he clambers in over the wheel. "I guess ye won't have any trouble in seein' it all 'fore sundown. I'll leave ye at the hall while I go down and take a look at the stock."

This style of family division is the rule of the day.

Of course the "main-stem" of all the New England fairs is the "hoss-trot." People sit patiently all the long hours of the afternoon on the crowded grand-stand, uttering no word of protest at the long delays and the tedious scorings and the backings and fillings for a start.

Picketed all over the inner oval are dozing Dobbins and umbrella-shaded sight-seers. All around the track the weather-worn rails are kneaded by the elbows of the gazing throngs. Fully half the crowd sees only the dizzy procession of sweating horses as they "racky-tack" past in a cloud of dust

and disappear around the turn. But that portion of the spectacle is satisfactory enough, apparently.

And all the long day the womenfolk crowd in procession through the aisles of the hall. They finger the log-cabin quilt, they speculate up on the number of stitches in the embroidery, and comment on the fact that Mis' So-and-So has brought that same old afghan to get another prize on it.

There are savory odors in the wing of the hall devoted to the cheeses and the honey and the butter and the home cooking. And what would a fair be without all the prizes of the gardens?

Down in the long sheds the wondering cattle hold court all day long and stick dewy and sweetly odorous noses out to meet the caressing hands of the passers. Even the pigs, snuffling in their troughs and grunting in mellow diapason, roll up their little twinkling eyes and hump up their fresh-scrubbed backs, sociably inviting a scratching when some jovial old farmer makes the rounds with a bit of shingle.

Actually, there isn't much at any New England fair that is novel and interesting if a person is looking for the marvelous. One fair is much like an-

It is the annual congress when the toilers can put away the cares for the day and meet with hearty hand grasp and swap stories.

other, and year after year, so long as they live, the same cows, the same oxen, the same horses fill the exhibition sheds, and yet the people come every year with just as keen zest. The explanation is that the people come to see each other.

And of course, to have a go at the games of chance. Why any one should hanker to throw baseballs at the woolly head of "Old Smoko, the Champion Dodger," isn't clear to many people who are not in sympathy with the fair spirit, and as to twirling a spindle over a numbered board, or ringing canes, or trying to knock over dummy dollies on a rail, or performing other animated stunts in order to win a few cigars that even the most rugged bucolic taste cannot endure once they are lighted—all that is a mystery to the persons who go home and say that the fair didn't amount to much.

Prize for the lady?

But all the folks that did those things, and did them the year before and will do them next year, they are the ones who kick off their dust-covered boots at night and shake the few remaining pennies out of their pockets and go contentedly to bed with the satisfaction of a well-spent day. (1903)

Fruit to fill a prize-winning pie, a well-earned day of fun and relaxation: the harvest of hard work.

The Hookers-Up

By SAMUEL G. BLYTHE

"Is it a club?" I asked the Man Who Had Been There Every Season for Ten Years.

"Is what a club?" he asked back, rather coldly, I thought.

"Why, this," I said, waving my hand comprehensively to include the porches, lobby and lawns.

"I do not understand," and there was no mistake about the ice.

"What I mean is this," I continued cautiously, for persons who have been there every season for ten years are of consequence and not to be trifled with or considered lightly: "Are all these apparently normal men wearing the same uniform because they belong to some club down here on an excursion, or something?"

"Uniform!" he exclaimed, congealing rapidly—he had just been explaining, with much detail, that he knew the hotel before they built the addition—"You jest. I see nobody wearing uniforms except the servants."

"Pardon me," I said, with that deference due to his position as one of the oldest guests, "but I can now see very plainly about two hundred men, all attired in blue serge coats, white flannel trousers, white shoes and straight-brimmed straw hats. If that isn't a uniform, what is it? Or," I suggested hopefully, "perhaps they are doing it on a bet?"

Well, he wore a blue serge coat, white flannel trousers, white shoes and a straw hat, and his low temperature was immediately dissipated by a hot wave he generated himself. He blew up.

Playing the game.

"Young man," he shouted, "that attire isn't a uniform—it is absurd—ridiculous—my word—I protest —uniform!—any person acquainted with the conventionalities of fashion would know that these garments"—he patted his blue serge coat and his white flannel trousers—beautifully creased—"why these garments are the only proper ones for morning wear at such a place as this. Uniform!!" He choked and spluttered into incoherence, trailing off into a stammering succession of "proper" —"fashion"—"conventional"—"my word" and "preposterous."

"What are you doing here?" I next asked him. "Are you here for a holiday?"

He straightened up. "I'm on my regular winter vacation. I have been here every

season for ten years. In fact"—and he was very proud about it—"I am one of the oldest patrons."

"And is it your idea of a vacation to come down here and rig yourself up every morning just like two hundred other people, or three hundred?"

"Young man," he said, and he was kind and patronizing now, "I fear you do not understand. It is proper, the proper thing. Why, I, myself bring twenty-seven pairs of white flannel trousers with me every time I come to Palm Beach."

Then he left me, and the procession of blue-serged and white-flanneled rest-seekers, young and old, moved slowly down to the end of one porch and back again, commented on by the countless blue-serged and white-flanneled rest-seekers who were in the chairs.

Surely, if one goes to Palm Beach one should do as the Palm Beachers do; else, why go? What profits it a person to pay eighteen dollars a day for a room unless he—and his wife—have the togs to make the splash? And what profits it a man—and his wife—to stay at Palm Beach after the splash is made? Move on, is the slogan; move on. Show all your clothes and pass along to the next stand. Climate? Perfect, but suddenly

imperfect if mamma has displayed every directoire she has in the trunk—oh, immediately too hot or too cold, and we must try it somewhere else. There is a subject for the investigator of natural phenomena: The Immediate Failure of the Climate of Palm Beach to Satisfy After the Tissue-Paper Has Been Taken Out of the Sleeves of the Last Evening Gown in the Trunk. It is sublime until that moment. Then it fails, fails miserably. Try it somewhere else? Certainly, for gowns can be shown again, you know, in a new hotel lobby, with all that grace and dignity that characterize the tourist lady, but never twice in the same place.

Primarily, one would think that when Papa and Mamma, for example, or Mamma and the Girls, or Jack and his Bride, go South in the winter it is to escape the rigors of the North—that's the accepted term—rigors of the North—fine, impressive language, too—enough to scare anyone into buying a ticket at once and, therefore, largely employed by the advertisers of the delights of the Sunny South—to escape the rigors of the North they would go for rest and recreation, to bask in the genial sunshine, any place where the basking is good, and loll under the palms, eating luscious, golden oranges, pitying

Friday's frock — soon to join Monday's through Thursday's at the bottom of the trunk — to be seen again only at the next resort.

those poor slaves of toil or fashion back home, condemned to follow the conventional paths of life and society. One would think that; but, dear brethren, the rigors of the North fade and faint into blessed balm when compared to the rigors of the South at a fashionable hotel.

Nature was lavish at Palm Beach before any but the Seminoles knew of it, and then came Henry M. Flagler, and he outlavished Nature ten to one, until he built a garden spot there beside Lake Worth as beautiful as a poet's dream. There is everything the heart of the seeker after rest could desire: a wonderful lagoon, a sapphire sea, the foliage of the tropics, sunshine for days and days, perfume-laden breezes, flowers, countless opportunities for rest and relaxation, luxury on every hand. It is every man's ideal.

But: "Now come along, John, it is time to change this breakfast frock for my morning gown and you must hook me up."

Hook her up! Many a tired and careworn citizen has spent several high-priced hours a

Chambermaids rush in where hookers-up revolt.

day hooking her up. Through the corridors of the hotels at breakfast time, at bathing time, at teatime and at dinnertime echo and re-echo: "Dod-gast it, I can't find the place for these hooks—why in thunder didn't that dressmaker put on a million of these things when she was about it?—keep your hands down by your sides, can't you?—how in blazes do you think I can get this thing shut if you go flowing yourself out like a pouter pigeon?—where in—where does this blamed thing go, anyhow?—there, I've busted two fingernails trying to squeeze you into this sausage case and I quit—I'm going home—go on and get the chambermaid, why don't you?—busy, is she, hooking up other women?—well, I'd think you'd have gumption enough to hire her, too—there—I don't give a hang if it is crooked—I'm through—do you understand that?—I'm through."

And then, too, in shriller tones: "Why, William, I am astonished at you—I—am—astonished—didn't come down here to wrap yourself in stiff shirts and put on evening clothes every night?—the idea—I'd look well, wouldn't I, with my new gown, going down there among all those people and you escorting me, still dressed in that old sack suit? —you have just got to do it.

"Why, William Jones, everybody does—wouldn't you cut a pretty figure down there in that lobby without a dress suit?—don't know any of them, you say?—what difference does that make—do you think I am going to be humiliated by sitting around with you, and every other man all dressed up?—I won't go down at all—sniff—now. Be a dear and go on and dress up—oh, and are you sure you hooked all the hooks?"

There are two times when you can escape, only two: the night when you arrive and the trunks are not yet up, and the night when you go away and the trunks are packed. Even then you go about telling your casual acquaintances, in the most casual way, but so they will understand why you are not rigged out, that you just got in and the trunks haven't arrived, or that you are leaving at midnight and the trunks have already gone to the train; in the most casual way, of course, but always, for it is inexorable at Palm Beach, inexorable.

It is a show place and you are part of the show. If you do not take your part you have offended against conventionalities, and can you imagine a baser thing than that to do, especially where you, although being part of the show, are paying for it?

Florida is a pleasant playground and its most beautiful spot is Palm Beach. There is boating

The sailor's togs.

there, and fishing, and bathing, and golf, and tennis, and all sorts of opportunities for enjoyment, and many of the regulars get the best out of it. But having made Palm Beach the show place it is, the people go down there mostly for the purpose of putting on a show. Some members of the cast play their parts with obvious enthusiasm. Others on the other hand, have to play their parts particularly well to guise their true feelings. The latter may think he came down to loaf, but he didn't. He came down to do as others do, and he'll do it too, or pass on to another place. Tuxedos are the thing. Lovely garments, too, with the thermometer along about eighty. Comfortable as Navajo blankets—almost.

The women like it, until they have exhibited all their clothes, and then they pass along. The men, the hookers-up, have to like it, whether they want to like it or not.

It is a wonderful show, a wonderful show of gorgeous gowns, of glittering jewels, of women brilliant in prevailing modes, of fashionable togs of all kinds; a wonderful show run on schedule every day, with only incidental regard for the sparkling lagoon, the sapphire sea, the perfumed breezes, the tropical foliage; with surprising little attention paid to those stately palms—the royal and the cocoa—but with careful consideration, if you would be at all happy, of that other ever popular variety of palm—that is the outstretched—that can be readily observed in great profusion. (1909)

The American Holiday

An EDITORIAL

There are in the United States nearly thirty holidays of one kind or another, but only five of them receive anything like general observance—Christmas, Thanksgiving Day, Election Day, Fourth of July and the Twenty-second of February. We have no national holiday, but by the proclamation of the President of the United States and the action of the different States we get something that resembles it. Washington's Birthday comes as near to a real recognition by the whole nation as any other, the only flaw. being that, in Mississippi, where there are no statutory holidays, it is observed only by exercises in the public schools. But the day itself stands forth unique and distinct as the nation's greatest tribute to any individual.

As time goes on we seem to be reaching a higher appreciation of Washington's character. We have had in the past decade numerous new books exploiting sides of his private life that belong more to yellow journalism than to literature, but the splendid point is that not even in their microscopic investigations have these writers found anything that detracts from the real elevation of the man. "America has furnished to the world the character of Washington. And if our American institutions had done nothing else, that alone would have entitled them to the respect of mankind," said Daniel Webster in his oration at Bunker Hill.

It has been smartly said

Originally "Grand Old Rag."

When in the course of human events. . .

that we have made of Washington a chromo [*chromolithograph*]. Certain it is that each time we go back to study his work and life we return refreshed with the nobility of plain, simple duty—duty not only in doing that which a man and a patriot should do, but in keeping himself clean and upright. "I hope," wrote Washington in his Moral Maxims, "I shall always possess firmness and virtue enough to maintain what I consider the most enviable of all titles, the character of an 'honest man.'"

He did that with absolute success, and he was enabled to do it by the observance of another of his maxims: "Associate with men of good quality if you esteem your own reputation, for it is better to be alone than in bad company."

With this vantage his life along these higher lines moved nobly to its goals. He knew misrepresentation and abuse of the most harrowing kind, but he kept on, and time cleared his good name of all the the stains that bad men sought to put upon it in the times of stress and passion.

We have on Christmas the opportunity for love and charity, at Thanksgiving the occasion for gratitude, on Election Day the right of self-government, on the Fourth of July the display of patriotism, and on the fifth of our great holidays comes the call for duty—duty as shown in the life of a great man who did his work well, and lived up to his ideals without shirking any task. (1903)

The Night Before Christmas

By CARL WERNER

Twas the night before Christmas, when all through the flat
Not a creature was stirring, not even the cat.
Above the steam-heater the stockings were placed
In hopes that by Santa they soon would be graced.
The children were snug in their wee folding-bed,
While visions of Teddy-bears danced through each head.
And I in pajamas—likewise in a grouch—
Had gone to my patent convertible couch,
When out on the asphalt there rose such a clatter,
I sprang from my bed to see what was the matter.
A mantle of darkness enshrouded the room,
The "quarter" gas meter had left us in gloom,
But, after detaching a chair from my feet,
I threw back the curtain, looked down the street.
The arc light shone bright on a new garbage-can
Awaiting the call of the D.S.C. man;
And what did my wondering optics devour
But a big touring-car of a hundred horse-power
With a businesslike chauffeur, so shiny and slick,
I knew in a jiffy it must be Saint Nick.
As dry leaves before the wild hurricane fly
He ascended the fire-escape—nimble and spry.
I drew in my head, and was turning around,
When in through the airshaft he came with a bound.
His coat was of broadcloth—the finest I've seen—
Though it smelled rather strongly of fresh gasoline.
A bundle of banknotes he had in a sack,
And he looked like a winner just home from the track.
His cheeks—were like roses, his nose—like a cherry;
He'd the air of a man who is satisfied—very!
A fragrant Perfecto he held in his teeth,
While its smoke crowned his ten-dollar tile [*sic*] like a wreath.
He had a broad face and a well-nourished belly
That shook, when he laughed, like a bowlful of jelly.
He was chubby and plump, but a shrewd-looking guy,
And there gleamed through his goggles a keen little eye.
He spoke not a word, but the foxy old elf
Just walked to the mantel and laid on the shelf
A letter, typewritten in businesslike style,
Then down the dumb-waiter he sped with a smile.
He jumped in his car, and with three loud "honk-honks,"
He whizzed 'round the corner and off toward the Bronx.
I opened the letter, the message I read,
And then I crawled silently back into bed;
For here's what I saw—with dismay and disgust:

"RETIRED FROM BUSINESS;
SOLD OUT TO
THE TRUST."
(1907)

Resembling more the tough tycoon than the jolly old elf, even Santa went for big business in 1907.

An Assault on April First

An EDITORIAL

It appears that the leading club women of a prominent Western city have pronounced against the pranks of All Fools' Day. These pleasantries, say the ladies, lack in real humor, and do nothing for the Betterment of the Race. Alas, one by one are the cherished institutions of the ages attacked! The only gleam of light in the darkness is the fact that these are the same ladies who early in February issued a manifesto against the comic valentine, the latter part of the month bringing a statement from the manufacturers of these works of art that sales were never larger.

Why do the ladies rage against the first of April? Could it be possible that they have been the victims of some of this humor which is not real

The foolishness of All Fools' Day! Is the bricklayer a toothless sprite or ruthless matron? Extraneous detail to the victim (and his toe).

humor? Or, worse yet, have they attempted some of this spurious humor which has failed? It is a sad thing to try to pick up a pocketbook just as it is jerked away by a string, but it is sadder still to carefully arrange such a masterpiece of humor and then to have the intended victim plant his foot on the string and with an unfeeling jeer cast the purse into the middle of the street.

But surely prominent club women, leaders of society, would never hide behind a lumber pile gleefully holding a pocketbook string while they waited for the principal of the school to come along. It is not so certain, however, that they might not on occasion essay the annexation of a strung purse, or take up one stringless but stuffed with sand and paper. Then, too, they may easily have fallen victims to the toothsome-looking doughnut harboring nothing but cotton-batting, or the pumpkin pie concocted of sawdust and soap.

But, after all, the cause of the ladies' action is of minor importance; the real point is, Is this the beginning of a movement which will sweep away another of childhood's delicious joys? It seems especially hard to think of giving up the ancient hat with the brick under it on the sidewalk. Here we have real humor; no club women shall tell us that it is not real; it is the true essence of humor, embodied, made concrete and manifest to the eye—and toe.

Besides, this is of real benefit to society; the leading citizen, perhaps grown haughty, purse-proud and overbearing, suffers a true chastening of the spirit and is a better man after he has kicked the ancient headgear in his arrogant way and found the brick. The memory of it goes with him through the year, and turns his thoughts to good works. Woman, spare April Fool Day; touch not a single joke! (1902) 🐦

The Arts

C Had critics been able to kill,
no masterpiece could have
survived. (1902)

What Art Needs is a Salesman

By JAMES L. FORD

One hears a great deal about the unfortunate conditions under which the arts of painting and sculpture carry on the struggle for an existence in this country, and it is generally considered that it is due to ignorance and lack of artistic perception on the part of the public that the sculptor and his brother of the brush do not enjoy prosperity as do the successful playwright, actor, and man of letters.

"What Art needs in America to-day is an elevated public taste," wail the philosophers of the commonplace with their usual capacity for not understanding a question. What Art really does need in this country is a good salesman, and until it can be put on as sound a commercial basis as the theatre or the book trade its followers will continue to wring their hands and deplore the lack of artistic atmosphere and public appreciation they ought to have.

The artist invariably grudges the percentage he must pay on a sale of his work, which is not to be wondered at when we consider how little is done, as a general thing, to earn that percentage. The dealer simply hires what he calls a "gallery" on Fifth Avenue, covers its walls with pictures which have been intrusted to him to sell on the percentage basis, and then lies in wait for his prey. He has not yet learned the art of newspaper booming which enters into every form of industry, and consequently the public knows nothing of the personal characteristics of even our most distinguished artists.

His front room is devoted to American landscapes, but he uses these only as a sort of "blind" for his real business, which is conducted in a back parlor hung with thick curtains and provided with the most elaborate contrivances for lighting and exhibiting pictures to the very best advantage. Visitors who are attracted by the exhibition in the show windows—for your true art dealer is also an expert "window dresser," as it is termed in the vernacular of the department store—enter the front room where they are permitted to examine the works of art at their leisure, while the dealer "sizes them up" and wonders what their chief weakness may be. If, prompted by an unusual interest in some landscape, they ask questions about it, the dealer shakes his head with a despondent smile. He knows nothing of the picture save that it was brought there by an American artist. Perhaps the ladies are interested in pictures? Yes! Then if they will step this way he will show them something that just arrived from Europe. It is the work of the brilliant young Dutch artist, Kersloop, of whom they have certainly heard. Such color! Such atmosphere!

To the artist it's the intrinsic value of man-made motion contrasted with wind as the pure element of Nature and practicality as the purpose of its function. To the prospective customer, it's a windmill.

And thus softly gabbling, he leads the way into the back room, the curtains close noiselessly behind them and a velvet-footed attendant places on an easel the Kersloop masterpiece, a windmill on a ditched and dyked plain with a gray farmhouse in the distance and two forlorn geese in the foreground. No humans—but his work shows "breadth of treatment," "mystic tenderness" and several things in Italian which sound very well.

After the bargain has been concluded the visitors depart through a side door so that there is no possibility of their seeing again or even remembering the American works of art with which the dealer baited his hook.

There is one thing, however, that the art dealer should do for his clients which is of far greater importance than newspaper puffery, and that is to furnish fuller information regarding the pictures that he offers for sale than he does now. We are essentially a practical-minded people, and the majority of us are more apt to buy a picture because of some personal interest in what it represents than because of the technical skill which, after all, only a very few of us can appreciate. The buyer who is not an art connoisseur is certain to ask questions about a picture that catches his fancy. Where was it painted?

Who is the man in the foreground? What sort of an old-fashioned machine is that by the roadside? They are the sort of questions that an artist would probably scorn to answer, but the best way to sell a picture is to make known all these details to the prospective buyer.

The sort of titles that artists bestow upon their works have been aptly characterized by Mr. Munkittrick in one of his poems:

> His "Digging Clams at Barnegat,"
>   His "When the Morning Smiled,"
> His "Seven Miles from Ararat,"
>   His "Portrait of a Child."

These titles represent precisely the amount of information concerning each picture that can be extracted from the average exhibition catalogue that sells for a quarter of a dollar. Let the manager of one of these art exhibitions print twenty lines of description for each picture instead of one and he will certainly reap his reward in a larger attendance and a much larger sale of pictures. (1903) 🌰

"Tulips" or "Portrait of a Dutch Girl" is not much in the way of explanation to the amateur buyer.

Snaring Song Birds

By OSCAR HAMMERSTEIN

On the first night that I produced *Samson and Delilah* in Philadelphia I saw, in the lobby of the opera house between the acts, a well-known criminal lawyer of that city. I knew him by reputation and he evidently knew me, for he approached me and said quite jauntily:

"I am enjoying myself tonight. The music is very catchy."

Now it takes a good deal to surprise me. Twenty-six years of contact with temperaments and conditions more or less artistic provides a strong antidote for shocks. I must confess, however, that his use of the word catchy in connection with a majestic and inspiring Biblical opera, presented on an elaborate scale, was something of a jolt to my composure.

I met that same man toward the end of the season on a night when I was producing *Pélleas et Mélisande*. Once more he made for me. This time, however, I got ready. I expected him to say the opera was a "peach" or a "corker," and I was prepared to let loose a fine lot of sarcasm. Instead, he remarked with thoughtful seriousness:

"*Pélleas* is a very fine work. The music is noble."

"Isn't it catchy?" I asked with a smile.

The man remembered his first comment, for he remarked: "I have reformed. You see, I have been going to the opera steadily."

As we conversed I found that he had not only been going to the opera but he had been listening atten-

Music is an integral part of American living, making the American the most discriminating music lover in the world.

tively; and he had been reading about music. I was delighted to hear him speak with musical correctness, enthusiasm and genuine interest. His original instinct was all right; all it needed was a little cultivation.

His case was typical. What happened to him has happened to many Americans. Their development into music-lovers and opera-goers is due to the fact that the American ear is—at least so it has always seemed to me—more susceptible to good music than any ear in the world.

Why is the American ear, so youthful in its artistic training and experience, more keenly appreciative of music than the European ear which has had centuries of great music?

Music is part of the home life of the American. An American family that does not boast of at least one member who can play on some kind of instrument, or sing something when a visitor comes to call, is lacking in social standing in the community, whether it be a city or a crossroads village.

On the other hand, this particular opportunity does not come to the average European, whose wage is smaller and whose idea of home comfort and culture is not so extensive as that of the American. He cannot afford to have a piano or a phonograph as readily as the American. Therefore, the European child, while growing up, lacks the effect of music in the home air.

Naturally the question

arises: Why has the American ear not been discovered before? Simply because it has not had, until lately, the opportunity for the enjoyment of great operas. The American got for years a large dose of commonplace ballads, cakewalk ditties and ragtime. Grand opera, except in New York and a few cities, was a great novelty. But as the melodious works of the masters came within the hearing of the American ear it was quick and keen to respond.

The American ear is, likewise, the most cosmopolitan in the world. One reason for this is that the Continental music-lover clings tenaciously to the operas of his own people. Thus his musical range is always restricted. The native American loves the operas of all nations, and he plays no racial favorites. He will hear *Lucia*, *Tosca*, *Thaïs* or *Tannhäuser* with equal pleasure. And for this same reason his musical knowledge is widening just as his musical ear is constantly growing.

DRAWN BY J. J. GOULD

The slightest change in the weather can strain the delicate voice of the song bird.

There is still another distinguishing quality to the American ear, and this lies in the fact that it will not be buncoed. It is as discriminating as it is quick. Some of the greatest artists that come to the United States do not make an overwhelming impression, especially at the start.

The fact of the matter is that the American ear, like the gentleman from Missouri, must be shown. It must hear for itself. It accepts nothing on faith. You can advertise in the papers that you have the greatest tenor on earth, but the American ear will wait, and reserve judgment until it has heard.

The average American does not realize that great artists are scarce. Europe must be combed with a fine-tooth comb to get them.

In grand opera, you must remember, you do not deal so much with people as you do with their emotions. The greater the artist, the greater his or her vocal chords and the more sensitive his or her temperament. None of the great stars will sing more than three times a week, or at most ten times a month. Some of them get fifteen hundred dollars a performance. A slight change in atmospheric conditions will cause them to be indisposed. In addition

Harmonizing the violin and cello with the oboe and harp could sometimes be easier than harmonizing the temperaments of the artists.

to the colossal financial risk the director has incessant mental worry. The direction of grand opera is the most terrific strain imaginable on the mind.

Since the American ear is the most keenly appreciative of all musical ears it follows that it is a tremendous task to keep it supplied with melody. The world-search for stars is one of the most difficult features of grand opera production. You must fairly sweep the musical heavens, and the difficulties, the entanglements and the embarrassments that you encounter in this performance are little short of amazing.

You get some idea of the difficulty of the task when I say that though there are a million singers in Europe, there are only a handful of stars. The job is to find these stars.

Though Europe is the home of grand opera you

do not always find the prizes in the stately opera houses of some great capital. My theory about locating stars is that you are more likely to find them in obscure places. Suppose I want a great contralto. I search in vain through France, Germany and Italy. I go to elaborate performances of opera in the big cities and I am about to leave in despair. Suddenly, I find the operatic jewel that I seek.

Here is a story that will show how my plan works: Last summer, while abroad on my annual search for stars, I heard that there was a noted basso singing in the opera house at Havre in France. I went down to hear him in a performance of *Messaline*, an opera that has not yet been sung in the United States.

The much-heralded basso was disappointing, but in the same cast was a contralto unknown to me. Her name was Margarita D'Alvarez. The moment I heard her voice I realized I was listening to a great artist.

"She must be mine," I said. I went to see her after the performance and told her that I wanted her for America. I found that she had been singing in Algiers, in Rouen, in Cairo and was as yet undiscovered. I had made a real artistic find, for great contraltos are rare.

Take the case of Madame Eva Grippon, my new dramatic soprano. Last summer I went to Budapest to get the opera, *The Violin Maker of Cremona*. While there I heard of a small opera house at Ofen, which is across the river from Budapest. My instinct for stars led me there. The opera was of the barn-storming variety; the bill was the ever-present *Cavalleria Rusticana*. But amid the encircling gloom of that performance one splendid soprano voice rose and thrilled me. I determined to get that voice. It was Madame Grippon's. I told Madame Grippon that I would pay her a dollar for every krone that she had been receiving; that each year I would double her salary. I made a five years' contract with her, and I consider her to be one of my

The opera—an opportunity to study the art of conversation along with the art of music.

most fortunate talent discoveries.

Another case is presented by my new tenor, Jean Deffault. He had been singing in Constantinople, Algiers and Paris, yet no one had paid any particular attention to him. I heard of him. He was at the time in Constantinople. I agreed to pay his fare to Paris if he would come and sing for me. He came and I realized at once that he was a real artist; and his success in my preliminary season has more than vindicated my faith in him.

I do not believe in hunting operatic stars with a brass band, nor do I go to agents. By means of musical papers and magazines I keep in touch with operatic affairs the world over. If a new singer has been discovered in Algiers I make a note of it; if a soprano has success in Marseille [*sic*] I remember it. Then, when I go to Europe each summer I have in my head a long list of people. I send each one a letter asking him or her to meet me by appointment. I engage a hall, and then sit in the auditorium alone and listen to the artist.

The case of Marguerita Sylva, my new American prima donna, shows another method that I employ in getting stars. Twelve years ago, when conducting the Olympia Theater in New York, Miss Sylva came to me and got an engagement. She was a young singer with little experience. Every year I had put on a special musical skit which I wrote myself, so I put her in one of these. Then I wrote special songs for her. At the end of that season she obtained a good comic-opera engagement. Later she went to Europe and began to study for grand opera. Each year when I went over I heard her and carefully watched her progress. When I heard her sing *Carmen* at the Opera Comique in Paris I realized that she had become a prima donna, and I engaged her for that role and others at my opera house.

Miss Sylva was one of the class of singers that I call observed ones. They are a group of women with dramatic and vocal talent who are studying here in my choruses or abroad at some opera. In other words, they are training to be prima donnas.

Development of the two-sided record in 1904 brought opera into the living room.

I have long had the feeling that the chorus was the best training for the prima donna. The trouble with the American girls who want to be grand-opera stars is that they study too long under teachers. The chorus is the place to learn the practical side of opera. There is a young American girl who has been in my chorus for three years who this year will be a prima donna. She achieved the prize that many American girls have believed could only be obtained after enduring the drudgery and hardship and privation of European opera houses. And she was paid all the time she was being trained.

The enormous cost of grand opera in money and toil and worry is the tribute we have to pay to the American ear. In four years my grand opera investments have aggregated four million dollars. This includes the cost of my opera houses in New York and Philadelphia and the productions. Yet the earnings represented by those four seasons consist of four storehouses filled with productions.

The greatest reward for all this is the fact that the American ear is becoming more delicate each year. (1909)

In the Face
of the Ridiculous

By JULIA MARLOWE

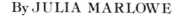

Julia Marlowe (born Sarah Frances Frost near Keswick, England in 1866) migrated with her family to the United States at an early age. Her first appearance on the New York stage in 1887 was a great success. In 1904, she joined E. H. Sothern, whom she later married, in a long-running series of Shakespearean plays. Best remembered for her moving portrayal of Juliet, Miss Marlowe left the stage in 1924 to spend her twilight years traveling with her husband.

I suppose it may be that inexplicable hysteria which sometimes lays hold of rational people and makes them laugh in church or even at a funeral service which also is accountable for the evil tricks a player's mind often serves him, causing him to laugh in the most serious and vital situation of a performance. You cannot say that such an incident is always the result of a highly developed sense of humor, because it is not always a really funny happening that will put a whole company to rout and drive sensible actors into gales of foolish, almost uncontrollable, mirth.

Julia Marlowe—accomplished actress and scholar.

Invariably it is in some fine, serious moment that these mad moods overtake one. The best one can hope for is, not to control a senseless impulse to laugh, but to seek refuge behind some other actor, or in a sheltered part of the stage, until the audience shall have ceased to notice that something had gone agley.

Of course, it is a lapsus linguae that usually furnishes the occasion for a stage contretemps and a hysterical panic in the ranks of the company. The

mistakes are frequently genuinely funny. Veteran actors take a certain pride in their stock of them, for more than one lapsus linguae has passed into stage tradition and become classic. The old-timers can quote you scores, ranging all the way from the "I dab thee with my stagger" of the eighteenth century player, who thus ruined the great scene of a fine tragedy upon the night of its initial production at Drury Lane, to the very latest slip of the tongue perpetrated yesterday by some matinee idol on Broadway. A slip of the tongue is a most demoralizing thing, in that the actor who has once made it never can speak the line again without a sickening apprehension that he is going to repeat the slip in spite of himself.

In *When Knighthood was in Flower* there is a line running: "A wild night for such a ride—a desperate venture!" The actor in whose part it was, slipped on it at the first reading, and made it: "A wild ride for such a night—a desperate venture!" and, pausing to correct it, he was interrupted by the stage manager, a veteran, with this warning: "No, never mind trying to change it now, for if you do you will always balk on the line and spoil the speech. It makes sense as you have it, so don't try to change it unless it comes perfectly natural the next time." So thoroughly did he realize the disconcerting nature of even a slight lapsus linguae upon a player when he sets out to mend the matter.

Perhaps one of the most trying contretemps that has occurred on the American stage in recent seasons overtook a sister artist of mine when she was giving the first performance of a serious and elaborate play, in an important American city. In the great emotional scene the sister of the character played by my friend falls at her feet in a passion of tears and entreaties. The heroine stoops to raise the stricken creature, and in tones that unite pleading and command cries: "Get up, Anne, get up!" On the evening in question one of that breed of imp-child, the gallery boy, amid the deathlike silence which followed the great outburst, clucked twice, after the manner of one starting a horse. It would have been a phenomenally self-restrained audience that could have resisted such a lapse from the sublime to the ridiculous. The scene went to pieces, the curtain was rung down, and the actress sought her dressing-room in a gale of hysterics.

I may add here that the gallery boy probably exerts, unconsciously, a wholesome restraint on both playwright and player. His sense of the ridiculous is positively gruesome, and no doubt it is the fear of some sacrilegious demonstration of his that keeps author and actor down to the level of sanity and warns them off the rocks of what Lowell denominated the "high-fa-lu-tin'" in literature and

A dramatic pose could become a fatal pause if interrupted by an outburst from the audience. The ability to recover well earmarks a top-notch performer.

art. Possibly for this reason, if for no other, he is to be tolerated. It is largely in deference to this patron of the drama that stage kisses must be exchanged, particularly in the serious moments of a play, with the utmost tact, grace and delicacy. Otherwise his sibilant pursing of the lips is likely to ruin your whole scene.

I have to confess that the extraneous influence which sometimes draws me out of the spirit of my part, and, once or twice, has made me laugh in the midst of a serious situation, arises from the fascination which faces of children in the audience have for me. I think perhaps few people realize how poignantly and completely every emotion children feel at a play is mirrored in their little countenances. I have seen them when their features seemed fairly wrinkled and knotted with the stress of their feelings. One small friend of mine occupied a box with his mother at a recent performance of *Knighthood*, and though he could not have understood very clearly the scene in which Mary is hunted from door to door of the ballroom of the Palais des Tournelles by King Francis, he did conceive that his friend Miss Marlowe was in some grave trouble. Suddenly he shot bolt upright in his chair and, with the quaintest little gesture of despair and anxiety that I ever saw, cried

Not visible to the naked eye, with or without opera glasses, are the goings-on in the wings: a real test for the actor on center stage.

out: "Mother, I can bear it no longer—I can bear it no longer!" Fortunately Brandon and Caskoden sprang through the secret panel at that instant and saved the day for Mary Tudor in more senses than one.

Rather disconcerting and certainly decidedly out of the picture was the spectacle which once greeted me in the tomb scene in *Romeo and Juliet*. Just as I spoke Juliet's piteous reproach over the lifeless body of her lover:

O churl! drunk all, and left no friendly drop
To help me after?

I happened to glance into the wings and, it being a Saturday matinée, I was mentally jerked out of Sweet Verona and into the prosaic present by seeing the treasurer of the company handing Friar Laurence the roll of bills that made up his weekly salary, that reverend worthy meanwhile lifting the skirts of his robe to tuck the money into his very nineteenth century trousers which he had put on under his priestly garments so that he could make a hurried exit from the theatre after the fall of the curtain. I then and there introduced a new bit of business into my interpretation of Juliet, and burying my head on Romeo's shoulder indulged in what I prayed the audience would believe was a passionate storm of sobs.

Other actresses besides myself have been completely upset in this same critical scene by the trick many Romeos have of falling on their dagger after the suicide in such a way that Juliet cannot reach the weapon to use it on herself. This is such a very important and trying scene that an actress' stage manager and maid usually stand in the wings watching her closely. If Romeo in his death throes does happen to lie with his dagger under him you can imagine what effect it must have on Juliet, who meanwhile is madly searching for the instrument, to hear her people in the wings whispering hoarsely, "Roll over, sir, roll over!" or "You idiot, hunch an inch up stage, so madam can get that knife."

The weird superstitions of stageland are accountable for many contretemps, and sometimes they are very serious ones. Some of the sanest and most brilliant players are devout believers in signs and omens. Possibly it is due to the unnatural and highly charged atmosphere in which they live, or it may be explained by the fact that so many successes and failures seem explicable only on the theory of supernatural interference. A trivial incident on the first night of a production may act upon people's nerves to such an extent that a highly important point in a play is lost or misinterpreted. Thereupon panic spreads through the company, the whole scene goes to pieces, and perhaps a production upon which thousands were expended passes into theatrical history as a failure. The incident which started the rout may have been so trivial that nobody can trace the way back to it. Hence the whole defeat is charged up to one of the thousand superstitions which flourish so luxuriantly amid the paint, powder and canvas of stageland. (1902) 🍇

Deadheads

By WALTER PRICHARD EATON

If a theatrical manager should put five hundred tickets into your hand one morning, saying: "Here are some seats for *The Girls of Goo-goo* tomorrow night; give 'em out to people who'll come and wear clothes that are at least decent"— what would you do?—that is, if for some strange reason you had to accept the task.

Perhaps you fancy it would be an easy job! But stop and think a moment. There is your family. Yes, they could use maybe six seats. The clerk in the office (you live in an apartment hotel, of course) can use two, surely; and the telephone switchboard girl is good for a couple more. The subway ticket-seller looks respectable, so you pass him over two, much to his amazement. On the train you rush up and down asking respectable-appearing people if they want to go to *The Girls of Goo-goo* tomorrow night. Some of them do, more don't. Some are insulted. Perhaps they've been already. You give away fifty tickets on the way downtown. You still have more than four

WANTED: Fans of another sort.

hundred tickets to *The Girls of Goo-goo* left.

All day long you offer to every one you meet, to every one who enters your office, to all the clerks and stenographers, two seats for *The Girls of Goo-goo*. By evening you are obsessed with the idea that you must give away seats to *The Girls of Goo-goo* to people who will promise to use them. You go to *The Girls of Goo-goo* yourself, finally, and after that you haven't the heart to offer more seats to anybody. At bedtime you count up your pack of pasteboards and find you still have over two hundred and fifty undistributed. You have miserably failed in your mission.

Yet it has become a part of the task of theatrical press agents in recent years, and more especially during this present season, to give away sometimes hundreds of tickets a week to the theaters under their charge, to "paper" their houses to an extent almost inconceivable to the general public, who suppose that theaters open only to the golden password. And they have been obliged to develop all sorts of expedients to bring about this wholesale distribution of passes. It is estimated on inside authority that in the thirty-odd "first-class" theaters in New York there might be counted at least six thousand deadheads on any Monday night this season—Monday night being the evening when paid attendance is always lightest. The various devices used by the managers to secure deadhead audiences when they cannot induce the paying kind to come make an interesting phase of theatrical life.

A year ago I sat at a performance, by Nazimova, of *The Master Builder*, and behind me sat two girls who chewed gum devotedly and endeavored to find out what the play was all about. From their conversation I gathered that they were parcel-wrappers in a Herald Square department store. After the second act one of them remarked to the other in an injured tone: "And Mr. Hawskell said this show was a comedy!"

"A bug-house funeral, *I* call it," was the reply.

The department stores are a boon to those who wish to fill up their theaters. Sometimes as many as two hundred seats for a single evening are sent in a block to the manager of a store, and he distributes

them to the girls. More often the distribution is made over a wider area, in smaller blocks. The telephone exchanges are useful places to the managers, the theory being that the girls will tell other people over the wire what a fine show they have seen. Just how far this theory is justified by the facts remains an open question. Your deadhead is often the deadliest knocker. All managers have a list of personal friends and "hangers-on" who may be relied upon to fill in. And the hotel clerks are frequent allies in the work of distribution.

There is one manager in New York who does not give free seats within the city limits, preferring to distribute them in the suburbs. He has a list of suburban residents, and these people are frequently astonished by receiving tickets to his theaters through the mail, with a little statement that Mr. — knows them to be influential citizens in their community and would like their opinion on his play. By the flattery, doubtless, Mr. — hopes to induce them to go back and spread kind reports of his attraction. One wonders if, perhaps, they don't spread reports of how they got the tickets, causing their neighbors to refrain from buying seats in the hope of similar blessings.

In the New York papers last fall a "want" advertisement appeared for girls to address envelopes. Applicants were to be at a certain theater on a certain morning. One of the applicants has narrated her experience. She entered the office to find a long line of girls ahead of her passing by a desk. The man at the desk seemed to be handing each girl a

*A "captivated" audience
is not necessarily kind.
A remedy for empty
seats—good plays.*

small envelope. When her turn came he stated that unfortunately all the vacant positions had been filled, but would she not accept two seats for the play downstairs that evening? Of course there had been no envelopes to address. The advertisement had been inserted in the papers solely to facilitate the distribution of tickets for a play that was an utter failure and which would, unless something desperate were done, be presented nightly to empty benches.

In plain language, there are more theaters in New York at present than there are good plays to adorn their stages and paying people to fill their plush chairs. The beginnings of the wholesale deadhead habit are to be found as far back, perhaps, as the old Union Square Theater days, when the line, One Hundred Nights in New York, became a valuable asset on the road. As the road tours of plays increased in length and the one-night stands multiplied, it became ever more important to a play if it could be advertised in advance as having run one hundred nights or more in New York. Therefore the managers began to force the runs of plays in the metropolis, began to keep them in town longer than actual business warranted. But if a drama played to empty benches after six weeks, news to that effect might conceivably spread aboard. If a visitor went back to Scranton and scattered the report that he had seen such and such a play in New York with twenty people for an audience, it might hurt the play when it reached Scranton. So the managers began to see to it that the house was never empty.

They have one perfectly good argument for so doing. A first-rate performance can probably never be given to empty benches. A bare theater chills the actors, deadens the whole tone of the performance; and that creates a bad impression on those who have paid real money to see the play. But the managers are beginning to feel that, perhaps, the counter arguments outweigh this one. By

To the satisfaction of theatergoers around the country, the successful play on tour is credited with "One Hundred Nights in New York."

ALONZO · KIMBALL

giving away so many seats persistently the managers are creating a great deadhead host out of potential paying guests. They are slowly killing the goose that once laid them golden eggs.

Every night at a theater, in the manager's little office, a process takes place at nine o'clock known as counting up. All the ticket stubs dropped by the door man into his box are dumped out and sorted into piles, which are carefully counted. One pile consists of the tickets sold for the full price, the other of the tickets which have been given away. The size of this latter pile, in almost every theater in New York this season, should give the managers food for thought. It might well inspire them with the reflection that perhaps they have built about all the theaters New York can support for a while. It might even lead them up to the brilliantly imaginative idea that they could wisely devote some of their energy to putting on better plays in those theaters they already have. If the deadhead can bring this happy result about he has not lived in vain. (1909)

Parting Words

By CORWIN KNAPP LINSON

I was closely associated with Stephen Crane during the years just preceding his success. It was a time when we both had our feet in the same Slough of Despond.

My first meeting with him was in the winter of 1892-3. One Sunday afternoon, Mr. Louis C. Senger, a cousin who was one of his intimates, brought him to my studio in the old building on West Thirtieth Street and Broadway. It was a dreary day, and the gray light filtered in through the cobwebby panes of the great sidelight, finding us in a kind of half-gloom. He talked little, sitting on a divan quietly smoking cigarettes. He impressed me as an unusual individuality, at first reserved, but soon expanding in the warmth of our comradeship.

It was a good beginning. His long rain-ulster became a familiar object, for those were slushy, drizzly days, and the winter air was oftener sleety with cold rain than fluffy with feathery snow.

My place was a black den and my affairs harmonized, so that it was quite a congenial retreat for Crane. It was his daily habit to come and compare notes. His facility used to astonish me. Sitting on my couch, rings of gray smoke circling about him, a pad on his knee, he would turn out a complete story in a half-hour. Sometimes it was a fragment that would be laid by for future use. Several sparkling sketches were invented and written in that atmosphere of melancholy, while I sat at my easel dabbling at a drawing and wondering how a new illustrator could get in his "wedge."

Crane had many loyal friends then, but, unfortunately, they were as poorly situated as himself:

Reading Civil War volumes for hours, Crane internalized impressions that became The Red Badge of Courage.

young doctors working out their hospital apprenticeships, boyish reporters and artists for obvious reasons unspoiled by prosperity; my cousin, who was none of these but equally at home with all; a half-dozen as ardent souls as ever banded together, to whom economy was at once a bugbear and a necessity. There were joyous days, and when fortune once sent us oysters and a beefsteak the notable occasion was duly celebrated.

We knew all the Cheap-John restaurants together. There was one to which many congenial spirits flitted on Saturday nights; where absolute liberty of emotion was allowed, where a tableful could break out into song and wild gayety without annoying any one particularly, where bad wine took the place of "draw one," and where the waiters conjured the knives, forks and spoons from the depths of cavernous breeches' pockets and wiped them on their sleeves! There could be no etiquette in a place like that, except that of good humor. We Americanized its French name into the Buffalo Mode, and once each week we carried our troubles to its murky atmosphere and joyous company. The life of our table—always the middle one of the room—was Crane, and the cheeriest sallies were from his lips.

In the spring of '93 Crane used to spend hours in my place rummaging through old periodicals, poring over the Civil War articles. I did not then grasp his drift, nor did he explain his interest in them. But he was sounding, trying to fathom the inwardness of war through the impressions on record, as I afterward understood. He did express some impatience with the writers, I remember.

"I wonder that some of those fellows don't tell how they *felt* in those scraps. They spout enough of what they *did*, but they're as emotionless as rocks."

He was evolving *The Red Badge of Courage*.

One evening he came to me, bringing several loose sheets of manuscript.

"What do you think I have been doing?"

"I can imagine anything, Steve."

"I've been writing—poetry!"

"Great Scott! let me see."

Well as I knew him, I was not prepared for what came. The sheets of legal-cap were handed over, and I read those marvelous short poems. I did not know how good they were. I confessed that they were something new to me, but that they made me see pictures, great pictures.

"Do they, honest?" delightedly.

I added that they moved me profoundly.

"Is that so?" seriously.

"Indeed they do, Steve, they're immense! How did you ever think of them?"

"They came."

That seemed to be the way of it, they just "came." And that was my introduction to his new character. I have two of those poems now.

It was not very long after that that an "Authors' Reading" was given, and my cousin Louis went with me, for some things from *The Black Riders and Other Lines* (still unpublished) were to be read. Far from reading his own work, at the idea of which he was aghast, Crane could not be induced even to go and hear—"would not be dragged by the neck"—so in dread was he of a misunderstanding of his work. He could stand up to adverse criticism like a catcher behind the bat, or retort to a gibe, giving better than he received—for his wit had a keen edge, and he was a master of repartee—but cold indifference was the "ax in the neck."

So he awaited our report in his room. We made it

The same character that explored and expressed the mood of the Civil War created "pictures, great pictures" with a unique form of poetry.

DRAWN BY GEORGE GIBBS

glowing, for the audience was enthusiastic and the *Lines* had been most effectively read by Mr. Barry.

The summer of '94 we were sent to do the mines at Scranton. It was Crane's first assignment from one of the magazines, but he had not enough money to pay his fare from New York. Luckily, I had enough just then to see us through, and we took

DRAWN BY W. F. BURGER

the offer joyfully. We were expecting after that to do the sea-divers, going down in diving rigs—but it did not happen.

After this, I saw less and less of him, for in '95 he made an extended tour through the West for a press syndicate, going into Mexico, and not returning for some months. Notes from the West and New Orleans were the only signs I had of his existence.

But he grew rich in material on this trip. He suddenly appeared one evening, and held me breathless with tales of adventure. One of them I saw afterward in print, but his vivid telling was so much more effective than even his pen-picture, that the written story seemed to lose color as I contrasted the two in my memory. That his luminous phrasing was not a trick was never more evident than then. It was simply Crane.

His speech was free from the danger that his writing ran, of weakening with repetition. Each scintillation eclipsed the last, but left a complete impression of delight.

Crane also covered the Spanish-American War from Cuba for the New York Journal.

He brought back a half-dozen opals, some with the lambent flame of the sunset in their fiery depths. He freely gave me the choice of the lot. I took a little one that flashed at me with the gleam of a rainbow. Crane laughingly added a fine water opal to it. The next morning he said:

"It's a good thing you came in for a deal yesterday, for the newspaper Indians gave me a dinner last night, and they got my pretty pebbles!"

I frankly regretted that I had made no better use of my opportunity!

And now—'96—our meetings grew less frequent. He spent much time away from New York, and I also was absent some months abroad. Finally he sent for a box of manuscript that had been some time in my care, and soon after unexpectedly showed himself at my door, just before his departure for Athens and the Greco-Turkish war. He was full of his prospective trip. It was a new phase of life, actual war, and the excitement of it was upon him. It was late when we parted, and it was my final "good-by."

And then a long blank, until, living in Paris, I heard of his illness in England, and before I could realize his condition the news of his death came.

It is inevitable that there must exist a nipping regret at the cutting off of a brilliant individuality in its early development. His was a cometlike career. And undeniably erratic and irresponsible in much as he was, he was lovable to a degree, daring and chivalrous, generous as the air, compelling a genuinely warm affection from those who best knew him; and for his genius I sometimes felt not a little awe, as for a power mysterious and unaccountable. (1903)

Other Lines

By STEPHEN CRANE

Crane's poetry—often regarded as eccentric—departed from traditional rhyme, rhythm and form. His unusual format (untitled works identified only by numerals) became a well-known trademark. In a mid-career evaluation, Crane said, "Personally, I like my little book of poems, *The Black Riders*, better than I do *The Red Badge of Courage*. The reason is, I suppose, that the former is the more ambitious effort. In it I aim to give my ideas of life as a whole, so far as I know it, and the latter is a mere episode, or rather an amplification."

1

Black riders came from the sea.
There was clang and clang of spear and shield,
And clash and clash of hoof and heel,
Wild shouts and the wave of hair
In the rush upon the wind:
Thus the ride of Sin.

2

I met a seer.
He held in his hands
The book of wisdom.
"Sir," I addressed him,
"Let me read."
"Child—" he began.
"Sir," I said,
"Think not that I am a child,
For already I know much
Of that which you hold.
Aye, much."

He smiled.
Then he opened the book
And held it before me.—
Strange that I should have grown so suddenly blind.

3

"Think as I think," said a man,
"Or you are abominably wicked,
You are a toad."

And after I had thought of it,
I said: "I will, then, be a toad."

4

The wayfarer
Perceiving the pathway to truth
Was struck with astonishment.
It was thickly grown with weeds.
"Ha," he said,
"I see that none has passed here
In a long time."
Later he saw that each weed
Was a singular knife.
"Well," he mumbled at last,
"Doubtless there are other roads."

5

There was a man with tongue of wood
Who essayed to sing,
And in truth it was lamentable
But there was one who heard
The clip-clapper of this tongue of wood
And knew what the man
Wished to sing,
And with that the singer was content.

6

I have seen thy face aflame
For love of me,
Thy fair arms go mad,
Thy lips tremble and mutter and rave.
And—surely—
This should leave a man content?
Thou lovest not me now,
But thou didst love me,
And in loving me once
Thou gavest me an eternal privilege,
For I can think of thee.

Mr. Kipling's New Book

By AGNES REPPLIER

It is a long time since we have had a book from Mr. Kipling's hands, and longer still since he has given us anything so fine as *Kim* (Doubleday, Page & Co.). He has written nothing better, and nothing, save the *Jungle Stories*, so good. He has returned for inspiration to the exhaustless East, and has woven from its web of wonders a tale wild as the Arabian Nights; a tale crammed with marvels, instinct with beauty, throbbing with life, and in which all the ordinary ingredients of fiction are conspicuously and delightfully absent. No time for sentimentalities and love-making in a narrative like this; no room for feminine petticoats in such crowded scenes; no chance at problem studying amid such a whirl of activities. Yet is Mr. Kipling's book as far removed from the ordinary "novel of incident" as Scott and Dumas are removed from the

Take an Irish orphan, raise him in India, school him in England, then cloak him in suspense—a tale only Kipling could tell.

harmless scribblers who water down their immortal stories into fiction gruel to-day.

If we want to read *Kim* in a spirit of unalloyed content we must accept its young hero without reserve or protest. An orphan waif, the son of an Irish soldier, but reared from infancy among the low-caste Hindus of Lahore, Kim's baby feet have trodden devious paths, his baby eyes have seen much that is commonly hidden from childhood. He is as acute as a young Hermes, as unscrupulous as a little Autolycus. A vagabond by instinct and by necessity, he attaches himself to a wandering Tibetan lama, and, in the capacity of chela, or disciple, follows the holy man in an endless search for the "River of the Arrow," the sacred river that washes away sin. The tale of their wanderings is the very cream of the book, for never were pictures of the Orient drawn with such brilliant colors, never were the shifting scenes incidental to pilgrimages all the world over described with such admirable art.

It is a veritable misfortune when Kim is picked up by his father's regiment, and sent, sorely against his will—and ours—to school. What has such an imp to do with desks and copybooks and grammars? His classroom is the world; his pedagogues, all things that walk thereon.

The story of the boy's training for the secret service is less convincing than the account of his childish adventures. It is hard to credit England with the wily depths of policy which Mr. Kipling describes. Indeed, even in Mr. Kipling's book, the Englishmen are singularly unimpressive; but of Mahbub Ali, the Afghan horse-dealer, and of Hurree Babu, the Bengali, one might believe anything. As for the Maharanee, she is simply the most delightful old woman we have met for many a year. If India holds many such grandmothers there is small need to vex our souls over the downtrodden females of the East. (1901)

Mrs. Loveredge Receives

By JEROME K. JEROME

The most popular member of the Autolycus Club was undoubtedly Joseph Loveredge. Small, chubby, clean-shaven, his somewhat longish soft brown hair parted in the middle, strangers fell into the error of assuming him to be younger than he really was. Guests to the Autolycus Club on being introduced to him would give him messages to take home to his father, with whom they remembered having been at school. This sort of thing might have annoyed any one with less sense of humor. Joseph Loveredge would tell such stories himself, keenly enjoying the jest—was even suspected of inventing some of the more improbable.

Another fact tending to the popularity of Joseph Loveredge among all classes, over and above his amiability, his wit, his genuine kindliness and never-failing fund of good stories, was that by care and inclination he had succeeded in remaining a bachelor. Many had been the attempts to capture him; nor with the passage of the years had interest in the sport shown any sign of diminution. Well over the frailties and distempers so dangerous to youth, of staid and sober habits, with an ever-increasing capital invested in sound securities, together with an ever-increasing income from his pen, with a tastefully furnished house overlooking Regent's Park, an excellent and devoted cook and housekeeper, and relatives mostly settled in the colonies, Joseph Loveredge, though inexperienced girls might pass him by with a contemptuous sniff, was recognized by ladies of maturer judgment as a prize not too often dangled before the eyes of spinsterhood.

Younger men stood by in envious admiration of the ease with which in five minutes he would establish himself on terms of cozy friendship with the brilliant beauty before whose gracious coldness they had stood shivering for months.

Joseph's lady friends might, roughly speaking, be divided into two groups: the unmarried, who wanted to marry him to themselves; the married, who wanted to marry him to somebody else. It would be a social disaster, the latter had agreed among themselves, that Joseph Loveredge should never wed.

Meanwhile Joseph Loveredge went undisturbed on his way. On a typical day, Joseph Loveredge left the house at nine-thirty for the office of the old-established evening paper, the *Good Humor*, that he edited. At one-forty-five, having left his office at one-thirty, Joseph Loveredge entered the Autolycus Club and sat down to luncheon. Everything else in Joseph's life was arranged with similar preciseness. On Tuesdays and Thursdays he was open to receive invitations out to dinner; on Wednesdays and Saturdays he invited four friends to dine with him at Regent's Park. On Sundays, whatever the season, Joseph Loveredge took an excursion into the country. He had his regular hours for reading, his regular hours for thinking. Whether in Fleet Street, or the Tyrol, on the Thames, or in the Vatican, you might recognize him from afar by his gray frock coat, his patent leather boots, his brown felt hat, his lavender tie. The man was a born bachelor. When the news of his engagement crept through the smoky portals of the Autolycus Club nobody believed it.

But the rumor grew into report, developed detail, lost all charm, expanded into

plain recital of fact. Joey had not been seen within the club for more than a week, in itself a deadly confirmation. The question became: who was she—what was she like?

"It's none of our set, or we should have heard something from her side before now," argued Somerville the Briefless.

"Some beastly kid who will invite us to dances and forget the supper," feared Johnny Bulstrode, commonly called the Babe. "Old men always fall in love with young girls."

"Forty," explained Peter Hope, editor and part proprietor of *Good Humor*, "is not old."

"I am hoping," said Peter, "it will be some sensible, pleasant woman, a little over thirty. He is a dear fellow, Loveredge; and forty is a very sensible age for a man to marry."

It was August. Joey went away for his holiday without again entering the club. The lady's name was Henrietta Elizabeth Doone. It was said by the *Morning Post* that she was connected with the Doones of Gloucestershire.

The marriage took place abroad, at the English Church at Montreux. Mr. and Mrs. Loveredge returned at the end of September. The Autolycus Club subscribed to send a present of a punch bowl, left cards, and waited with curiosity to see the bride. But no invitation arrived. Nor for a month was Joey himself seen within the club. Then one foggy afternoon, waking after a doze, with a cold cigar in his mouth, Jack Herring noticed he was not the only occupant of the smoking-room. In a far

Autolycus (as in the club) was a wily thief who could render his plunder invisible. Rules for membership had changed by 1904. . .or had they?

corner near a window sat Joseph Loveredge reading a magazine. Jack Herring rubbed his eyes, then rose and crossed the room.

"I thought at first," explained Jack Herring, recounting the incident later in the evening, "that I must be dreaming. There he sat, drinking his five o'clock whisky and soda, the same Joey Loveredge I had known for fifteen years: yet not the same. Not a feature altered, not a hair on his head changed, yet the whole face was different; the same body, the same clothes, but another man. We talked for half an hour; and he remembered everything that Joey Loveredge had known. I couldn't understand it. Then as the clock struck, and he rose saying he must be home at half-past five, the explanation suddenly occurred to me: *Joey Loveredge was dead: this was a married man.*"

"We want to know what you talked about," said Somerville the Briefless. "Dead or married, the man who can drink whisky and soda must be held responsible for his actions. What's the little beggar mean by cutting us all in this way? Did he ask after any of us? Did he leave any message for any of us? Did he invite any of us to come and see him?"

"Yes, he did ask after nearly everybody; I was coming to that. But he didn't leave any message. I didn't gather that he was pining for old relationships with any of us."

"Well, I shall go round to the office to-morrow morning," said Somerville the Briefless, "and force my way in if necessary. This is getting mysterious."

But Somerville returned only to puzzle the Autolycus Club still further. Joey had received with unfeigned interest all gossip concerning his old friends; but about himself, his wife, nothing had been gleaned. Mrs. Loveredge was well; Mrs. Loveredge's relatives were also well. But at present, Mrs. Loveredge was not receiving.

Members of the Autolycus Club with time upon their hands took up the business of private detectives. Mrs. Loveredge turned out to be a handsome, well-dressed lady of about thirty, as Peter Hope had desired. Jack Herring, as the oldest friend, urged by the other members, took the bull by the horns, and called boldly. On neither occasion was Mrs. Loveredge at home.

"I'm dashed if I go again!" said Jack. "She was in the second time, I know. I watched her into the house. Confound the stuck-up pair of them!"

Bewilderment gave place to indignation. Peter Hope one afternoon found Joey at the club, standing with his hands in his pockets, looking out of a window. So Peter, who hated mysteries, stepped forward with a determined air and clapped Joey on the shoulder.

"I want to know, Joey," said Peter. "I want to know whether I am to go on liking you, or whether I've got to think poorly of you. Out with it."

Joey turned to him a face so full of misery that Peter's heart was touched. "You can't tell how wretched it makes me," said Joey. "I didn't know it was possible to feel so uncomfortable as I have felt during these last three months."

"It's the wife, I suppose," suggested Peter.

"She's a dear girl. She has only one fault."

"It's a pretty big one! What is her objection to us? We are clean, we are fairly intelligent——"

"My dear Peter, do you think I haven't said all that and a hundred things more. A woman! she gets an idea into her head, and every argument against it hammers it in farther. She has gained her notion of what she calls Bohemia from the comic journals. It's our own fault; we have done it ourselves. There's no persuading her that it's a libel."

"Won't she see a few of us—judge for herself?"

"It isn't only that," explained Joey; "she has ambitions, social ambitions. Between ourselves, my wife is a charming woman. I'm in love with her just as she is, and always shall be. You don't know her."

"Doesn't seem much chance of my ever doing so," laughed Peter. "Are you going to give up all your old friends?"

"Don't suggest it," pleaded the little man. "You don't know how miserable it makes me, the mere idea. Tell them to be patient. The secret of dealing with women, I have found, is to do nothing rashly." The clock struck five. "I must go now," said Joey. "Don't misjudge her, Peter, and don't let the others. She's a dear girl. You'll like her, all of you, when you know her."

Peter did his best that evening to explain the true position of affairs without imputing snobbery to Mrs. Loveredge. It was a difficult task, and Peter cannot be said to have accomplished it successfully. Anger at Joey gave place to pity. The members of the Autolycus Club also experienced a little irritation on their own account.

"What does the woman take us for?" demanded Somerville the Briefless. "Doesn't she know that we lunch with real actors and actresses, that once a year we are invited to dine at the Mansion House?"

"Has she never heard of the aristocracy of genius?" demanded Alexander the Poet.

Jack Herring said nothing—seemed thoughtful.

The next morning Jack Herring, still thoughtful,

called at the offices of the *Good Humor* in Crane Court, and borrowed from Miss Bagshot, the society journalist, a copy of the "Debrett" [*the London social register*]. Three days later Jack Herring informed the club, casually, that he had dined the night before with Mr. and Mrs. Loveredge. The club gave Jack Herring politely to understand that they regarded him as a liar.

Somerville the Briefless called at the offices of *Good Humor* in Crane Court the following morning, and he also borrowed Miss Bagshot's "Debrett."

"What's the meaning of it?" demanded Tommy, the sub-editor.

"Meaning of what?"

"Well, Herring was here last week poring over that book for an hour with the *Morning Post* spread out before him. Now you're doing the same thing."

"Ah, Jack Herring, was he? I thought as much. Don't talk about it, Tommy. I'll tell you later."

On the following Monday the Briefless one announced to the club that he had received an invitation to dine at the Loveredges' on the following Wednesday.

One morning toward the end of the week, Joseph Loveredge, looking twenty years younger than when Peter had last seen him, dropped in at the editorial office of *Good Humor*, and demanded of Peter Hope how he felt and what he thought of the weather. Peter Hope expressed his determination not to be surprised should it even turn to rain.

"I want you to dine with us on Sunday," said Joseph Loveredge. "Jack Herring will be there. You might bring Tommy with you."

Peter Hope gulped down his astonishment, and said he should be delighted; he thought that Tommy also was disengaged. "Mrs. Loveredge will be out of town, I presume?" questioned Peter Hope.

"On the contrary," replied Joseph Loveredge, "I want you to meet her.

"Don't if you don't like," Loveredge continued, "but if you don't mind, why not call yourself, say, the Duke of Warrington."

"Say the what of what?" demanded Peter Hope.

"The Duke of Warrington," repeated Joey. "We are rather short of Dukes. Tommy can be the Lady Adelaide, your daughter."

"Don't be an ass!" said Peter Hope.

"I'm not an ass," Joseph Loveredge assured him. "He is wintering in Egypt. You have run back for a week to attend to business. There is no Lady Adelaide, so that's quite simple."

"But what in the name of——" began Peter Hope.

"Don't you see what I'm driving at?" persisted Joey. "It was Jack's idea at the beginning. I was frightened myself at first, but it is working to perfection. She sees you, ánd sees that you are a gentleman. When the truth comes out, as of course it must later, the laugh will be against her.

"I am risking something, I know," continued Joey, "but it's worth it. I couldn't have existed much longer. We go slowly and are very careful. Jack poses as Lord Mount-Primrose, who has taken up with anti-vaccination, and who never goes out into Society. Somerville is Sir Francis Baldwin, the great authority on centipedes. The Wee Laddie is coming next week as Lord Garrick, who married that dancing girl, Prissy something, and started a furniture shop in Bond Street. I had some difficulty at first; she wanted to send out paragraphs, but I explained that was only done by vulgar persons—that

Is he Sir, Lord or Duke? For sure. . .he is a gentleman.

when the nobility came to you as friends it was considered bad taste. She is a dear girl, as I have always told you. And any one easier to deceive one could not wish for. I don't myself see why the truth ever need come out."

"Well, it's your murder," commented Peter. "If you are willing to take the chances——"

"That's all right," responded Joey. "Then you'll come? He's about your age, a young-looking man for his years. Eight o'clock, plain evening dress."

"And Tommy is the Lady——"

"Adelaide. Let her have a taste for literature, then she needn't wear gloves. I know she hates them." Joey turned to go.

"Am I married?" asked Peter.

Joey paused. "I should avoid all reference to your matrimonial affairs," was Joey's advice. "You didn't come out of that affair too well."

"I'd have liked to have been some one a trifle more respectable," grumbled Peter.

"We rather wanted a Duke," explained Joey. "He was the only one that fitted in all round!"

The dinner was a complete success. Tommy, entering into the spirit of the thing, bought a new pair of open-work stockings and assumed a languid drawl. Peter, who was growing forgetful, introduced her as the Lady Alexandra: it did not seem to matter, both beginning with an A. She greeted Lord Mount-Primrose as "Billy," and asked affectionately after his mother. Joey told his raciest stories. The Duke of Warrington called everybody by their Christian names, and seemed well acquainted with Bohemian Society: a more amiable nobleman it would have been impossible to discover. The hostess was the personification of gracious devotion.

Other little dinners, equally successful, followed. Joey's acquaintanceship appeared to be confined exclusively to the higher circles of the British aristocracy, with one exception—that of a German Baron. Mrs. Loveredge wondered why her husband had not introduced them sooner, but was too blissful to be suspicious.

All might have gone well to the end of time if only Mrs. Loveredge had left all social arrangements in the hands of her husband—had not sought to aid his efforts. To a certain political garden party one day in the height of the season were invited Joseph Love-

Mrs. Loveredge—accustomed to Bohemian society.

redge, editor, and Mrs. Joseph Loveredge, his wife. Mr. Joseph Loveredge at the last moment found himself unable to attend. Mrs. Joseph Loveredge went alone, met there various members of the British aristocracy. Mrs. Joseph Loveredge, accustomed to friendship with the aristocracy, felt at her ease, and was natural and agreeable. The wife of an eminent Peer talked to her and liked her. It occurred to Mrs. Joseph Loveredge that this lady might be induced to visit her house in Regent's Park, there to mingle with those of her own class.

"Lord Mount-Primrose, the Duke of Warrington, and a few others will be dining with us on Sunday next," suggested Mrs. Loveredge; "will you not do us the honor of coming? We are only simple folk ourselves, but somehow people seem to like us."

The wife of the eminent Peer looked at Mrs. Loveredge, looked round the grounds, looked at Mrs. Loveredge again, and said she should like to come. Mrs. Joseph Loveredge intended at first to tell her husband of her success; but a little devil entering into her head and telling her it would be amusing, she resolved to keep it as a surprise to be sprung upon him at eight o'clock on Sunday. The surprise proved all she could have hoped for.

The Duke of Warrington, having journalistic matters to discuss with Joseph Loveredge, arrived at half-past seven, wearing on his shirt-front a silver star, purchased in Eagle Street the day before for eight and six. The Lady Alexandra accompanied him. Lord Garrick arrived with his wife (Miss Bagshot) on foot, at a quarter to eight. Lord Mount-Primrose, together with Sir Francis Baldwin, dashed up in a hansom at seven-fifty. The Honorable Harry Sykes (commonly called "the Babe") was ushered in five minutes later. The noble company assembled in the drawing-room, chatted blithely while waiting for dinner to be announced. The Duke of Warrington was telling an anecdote about a cat, which nobody appeared to believe—when the door was thrown open and Willis announced the Lady Mary Sutton.

Mr. Joseph Loveredge, who was sitting near the fire, rose up. Lord Mount-Primrose, who was standing near the piano, sat down. The Lady Mary Sutton paused in the doorway. Mrs. Loveredge crossed the room to greet her.

"Let me introduce you to my husband," said Mrs. Loveredge. "Joey, my dear, the Lady Mary Sutton. I met the Lady Mary at the O'Meyers' the other day, and she was good enough to accept my invitation. I forgot to tell you." Mr. Loveredge said he was delighted; after which, although as a rule a chatty man, he seemed to have nothing else to say. And a silence fell.

Somerville the Briefless—till then—walked up and held out his hand. That evening has always been reckoned the starting point of his career. Up till then nobody thought he had much in him.

"You don't remember me, Lady Mary," he said. "I met you some years ago; we had a most interesting conversation—Sir Francis Baldwin."

The Lady Mary took the hand held out to her. "Of course," said the Lady Mary; "how stupid of me. It was the day of my own wedding, too. You really must

The Lady Mary— held her head as high as her rank.

forgive me. We spoke of quite a lot of things. I remember now."

The announcement of dinner, as everybody felt, came none too soon.

It was not a merry feast. Joey told but one story; he told it three times, and twice left out the point. Lady Alexandra's behavior appeared to Mrs. Loveredge not altogether well bred. Every few minutes she buried her face in her serviette, and shook violently, emitting stifled sounds, apparently those of acute physical pain. Mrs. Loveredge hoped she was not feeling ill, but the Lady Alexandra appeared incapable of coherent reply. Twice during the meal the Duke of Warrington rose from the table and began wandering round the room looking for his snuff-box. The only person who seemingly enjoyed the dinner was the Lady Mary Sutton.

The ladies retired upstairs into the drawing-room. The entire male portion of the party crept on tiptoe into Joey's study. Joey, unlocking the bookcase, took out his "Debrett," but appeared incapable of understanding it. Sir Francis Baldwin took it from his unresisting hands; the remaining aristocracy huddled themselves together into a corner, and waited in silence.

"I think I've got it all clearly," announced Sir Francis Baldwin, after five minutes, which to the others had been an hour. "Yes, I don't think I'm making any mistake. She's the daughter of the Duke of Truro, married in fifty-three the Duke of Warrington, at St. Peter's, Eaton Square; gave birth in fifty-five to a daughter, the Lady Grace Alexandra Warberton Sutton, which makes the child just thirteen. In sixty-three, she divorced the Duke of Warrington. Lord Mount-Primrose, so far as I can make out, must be her

The assumption of Lady Garrick's title conveyed none of her accomplishments as a pianist to Miss Bagshot.

second cousin. I appear to have married her in sixty-six, at Hastings. It doesn't seem to me that we could have got together a homelier little party to meet her even if we had wanted to."

Nobody spoke; nobody had anything particular worth saying. The door opened and the Lady Alexandra (otherwise Tommy) entered the room.

"Isn't it time," suggested the Lady Alexandra, "that some of you came upstairs?"

"I was thinking myself," explained Joey, the host, with a grim smile, "it was about time that I went out and drowned myself."

"Come upstairs, all of you," insisted Tommy, "and make yourselves agreeable. She's going in a quarter of an hour."

Six silent men, the host leading, the two husbands bringing up the rear, went up the stairs, each with the sensation of being twice his usual weight. Six silent men entered the drawing-room and sat down on chairs. Six silent men tried to think of something interesting to say.

Miss Bagshot—it was that or hysterics, as she after-ward explained—stifling a sob, opened the piano. Miss Bagshot was a poor performer at the best of times, and the only thing she could remember was "Champagne Charlie is my Name," a song then popular in the Halls. Five men, when she had finished, begged her to go on. Miss Bagshot explained it was the only tune she knew. Four of them begged her to play it again. Miss Bagshot played it a second time, with involuntary variations.

The Lady Mary's carriage was announced by the imperturbable Willis. The party, with the exception of the Lady Mary and the hostess, suppressed with difficulty an inclination to burst into a cheer. The Lady Mary thanked Mrs. Loveredge for a most interesting evening, and beckoned Tommy to accompany her. With her disappearance, a wild hilarity, uncanny in its suddenness, took possession of those remaining.

A few days later the Lady Mary's carriage again drew up before the little house in Regent's Park. Mrs. Loveredge, fortunately, was at home. The carriage remained waiting for quite a long time. Mrs. Loveredge, after it was gone, locked herself in her own room. The under-housemaid reported to the kitchen that passing the door she had detected sounds indicative of strong emotion.

Through what ordeal Joseph Loveredge passed was never known. For a few weeks the Autolycus Club missed him. Then gradually, things righted themselves. Joseph Loveredge received his old friends; his friends received Joseph Loveredge. Mrs. Loveredge, as a hostess, came to have only one failing: a marked coldness of demeanor toward all people with titles. (1904) 🦂

All it took was one surprise to open Mrs. Loveredge's eyes.

The World

A Game for an Empire
By Senator Albert J. Beveridge

⊄In the fable the wolf called the ox a robber.
In the modern version they get together
and form a trust. (1903)

Campaigns, Candidates and Coming Trends

An OVERVIEW

Incomparable Amusement

An EDITORIAL

With a record-setting majority of votes, Republican candidate Teddy Roosevelt beat Democratic nominee Alton B. Parker in the 1904 presidential election.

We are about to enjoy again the most absorbing of all American pastimes—a hotly contested Presidential campaign. There were elections in 1896 and in 1900, but there was too little doubt about the result to make the contests interesting. Besides, so many Democrats voted for Republicans that there was really no direct party issue.

This year party lines will be drawn as they have not been drawn since 1892; and a natural result of a vigorously fought campaign will be an immense increase in the vote. Between 1896 and 1900 the total vote remained almost stationary—13,923,378 in the former year; 13,961,566 in the latter. This was due principally to the decline in voting in the South, but there were also decreases in the votes of Maine, Michigan, Minnesota, Nevada, Oregon, Pennsylvania, Vermont and Wisconsin. This year it is hardly to be doubted that the voters will turn out at least fifteen millions strong. The battle will rage in every Northern State except Vermont, for even in Pennsylvania the Democrats will have hopes of making gains in Congress.

Some persons find excitement in baseball, others in horse-races, but there is nothing that can keep the whole nation in one prolonged nervous thrill like an old-fashioned Presidential campaign. No other people has anything to compare with it. In every other great country a "general election" is merely the choice of members of Parliament. Here it is a colossal duel between two matched champions. From July to November even the war news will be an "inside-page story" compared with this overshadowing contest. (1904) 🐾

Knowing the Candidates

An EDITORIAL

American politics will never be altogether right so long as the unknown man makes the strongest candidate. (1901)

It was long an obvious disadvantage that, in local elections in cities, no one knew anything about the men he was voting for, excepting the candidates for two or three higher offices upon whom the newspapers centred attention.

Decent government began in Chicago with the Municipal Voters' League, an independent, militant organization which made a business of telling ward residents about the records and reputations of aldermanic candidates. Elsewhere, now, there are

useful associations which perform the same function, and it is not so easy for a professional pickpocket to get elected to a position of trust with the facile aid of a party indorsement.

This growing scrutiny of the lesser candidates is highly valuable. The general fault, we think, is that it often puts a too exclusive emphasis upon mere honesty. What brings this especially to mind is the result, so far, of the inquiry into graft in the building of the Pennsylvania State Capitol.

Governor Pennypacker, we hear, is a very honest man. Whether the gentlemen who were looting the treasury under his nose could, by any mathematical or physical possibility, have stolen more if his moral qualities had been less, is doubtful. They seem to have taken everything in sight. The Governor's honesty was valuable for his personal salvation. What good it did the State does not appear.

In the past, a man long in the public service has been impugned. With the growing change in the method of selecting public servants and the slow relegation to the background of the party machine, comes a change in this sentiment. We are prepared to see in time a professional class of office-holders—who must be competent as well as honest to keep their jobs. (1907) 🐛

A Look Ahead in Politics

An EDITORIAL

WHICH?

Not since the Civil War have all branches of the National Government been so fully under the control of one political party as they are now under that of the Republicans. Everything is in their hands. Congress is thus classified in the latest edition of the Congressional Directory: Senate—Republicans 54, Democrats 30, all others 6; House of Representatives—Republicans 200, Democrats 152, all others 5. All the committees are heavily Republican and the minorities of both bodies are practically helpless.

We have, therefore, several years of assured Republican administration ahead of us. This, however, does not prevent the raising of new questions upon which political battles may be fought. One will be on the growth of trusts and other vast combinations of wealth. Another will be on the tendency to acquire more territory—a tendency somewhat ambiguously called imperialism. Still another will be on the tariff, and that in all likelihood will develop into the most important of all. The growth of the Government and the necessary increase in its expenditures will supply some very imposing statistics for campaign use, and there will be plenty of eloquence one way and another on freedom for the Filipinos.

Perhaps the greatest gratification in our politics is the fact that cleaner methods are used. The virulent personal abuse which was so disgraceful a few years ago has gone, never to return. The man who would try to revive it would lose the respect of his own adherents. Thus we are getting away from personalities and nearer to the ideal discussion of politics and principles. We can look forward to political contests with an assurance of interest without the stain of slander. (1901) 🐛

Man of the Decade, Talk of the Times

By JOHN T. McCUTCHEON

Under the shadow of a heavy sorrow, the assassination of President William McKinley, the Nation greets President Roosevelt. Younger than any man who before has held the Presidency of the United States, our new Chief Magistrate has on that account a fuller measure of the Nation's sympathy. Honest, personally brave, of a sincere Americanism, the Nation looks to him to lead it further in its career of honorable glory, of honorable success.

Assuming his high office in a time of National grief, and under painful and delicate circumstances, all classes, all parties, all sections freely offer him their sympathy, their confidence, their encouragement.

The assassination of President McKinley has stirred the Nation to its depths. But while it is still sorrowing over the tragedy that has passed, it sees hope for continued prosperity, for continued National progress, in the accession of a man who has been tried in the balance of high office, who is conversant with important public affairs, and whose record thus far has been one of achievement and activity. (1901)

The historian of the future who delves through the newspaper files of the years 1900 to 1909, inclusive, will come to one inevitable conclusion about early twentieth-century America.

Teddy and his trademarks.

He will conclude that the most important news of that period was Mr. Theodore Roosevelt, President, politician, statesman, sociologist, reformer, defender of the faithful, exposer of shams, protagonist, antagonist, hunter, diplomat, apostle of Peace, and wielder of the Big Stick. He may also conclude that Mr.

Roosevelt was both an Imperialist and a Socialist, and, perhaps, a Democrat and a Republican. The things that Mr. Roosevelt has said and done, and, particularly, the way he has said and done them, have made him an inexhaustible Golconda of inspiration for the cartoonist.

It may not be too much to say that much of Mr. Roosevelt's celebrity has been due to the fondness of cartoonists in picturing him. His teeth and eyeglasses became famous almost before he himself did. When he smiled it suggested a man in ambush behind a stone wall. His personal appearance was "catchy" as well as absolutely unique, and when, in addition, the great public heard that his name was "Teddy," the combination was one that tickled the popular fancy through and through.

To New York State he was undoubtedly well known long before the country at large became interested in him. As a legislator, police commissioner, and whatever else he may have been in New York, he was probably known to many people as an aggressive "comer" of the live-wire kind. As civil service commissioner he began to extend his fame beyond the borders of his own section, and, one might say, "carried a spear" in the national drama.

Then, all of a sudden, like the bursting of a rocket that showers red, white and blue stars in the sky, the nation, as one man, was talking about Teddy Roosevelt's Rough Riders. The very idea of a regiment of cowboys, collegians, gun-fighters, cotillon-leaders, millionaires and plainsmen smacked of daring and dash and chivalry, like the Black Horse Brigade and Morgan's Raiders. The moment the words "Rough Riders" appeared in the press, their fame was assured.

Many Presidents of the past have allowed their mental processes to operate in a limited orbit, touching only the weighty problems of statecraft and diplomacy. Not so Mr. Roosevelt! No class of people, no subject, has been too humble for his absorbed attention. "How to make farm life more attractive to boys" came in for the same eager consideration as the most direct method of insuring the construction of a many-million-dollar canal.

As a coiner of words and a doctor of phraseology he is supreme. The word "strenuous" has become a household word, practically coexistent with Mr. Roosevelt's regime, although the word has slumbered in the lexicons for ages. "Mollycoddle" tickled the ear and would not be forgotten. "Swollen fortunes," "malefactors of great wealth," "the predatory rich," "muckrakers," "a soft word and a big stick," "tainted money," "de-lighted," "the crop of children is the best crop of a nation," and hundreds of other expressions that have leaped into favor like the words of a popular jingle, owe their vogue to his instinct as a promoter and advertiser.

My own experience as a cartoon chronicler of Mr. Roosevelt extends back only to 1900. He had just been nominated for Vice-President, having been "kicked upstairs" by his political enemies, who sought to get rid of him by making him the vermiform appendix of our Government. In most of the cartoons of this period the Rough Rider type of military hero is used to symbolize him.

In 1901, acting more as an executor of Mr. McKinley's policies than as a proponent of new ones of his own, we find that he inspired comparatively few cartoon ideas. His volcanic

energy was in leash. But in January, 1902, his initiative began to assert itself once more, and in consequence of it he soon became embroiled with Congress, with the result that the latter dumped the Panama Canal problem on his hands and told him to settle it the best way he could. His method was direct, unparliamentary and effective.

In June of 1902, Judge Taft first appeared with Mr. Roosevelt in the cartoons. The President, attired in the newly-won robes of an LL.D., was represented in the act of conferring degrees upon his most faithful lieutenants, Judge Taft receiving the degree of Doctor of Benevolent Assimilation in recognition of his splendid work in the Philippines, Secretary Root the degree of Doctor of War, and General Wood the degree of Doctor of Diplomacy.

In that same year Oyster Bay was added to the assets of the cartoonist. Hitherto it had won no particular identity as a geographic center, but when the new President made it his summer capital it burst into a sudden, garrulous importance that made its humble name a misnomer. Here the President went for rest and quiet, but, if he got relief, it was not from the cartoonists. Every detail of his daily life was duly cartooned, largely from imagination, and spread to the winds. Even the visitors that swarmed to Oyster Bay drove the humorists of the pencil to extremes of activity. There was an amazing variety of visitors, you may be sure, and they ranged throughout the entire gamut of humanity. For instance, on Monday, the President entertained the champion tennis player; on Tuesday, some old Rough Rider friends; on Wednesday, some fellow LL.D.'s; on Thursday, a

A presidential name-sake lives on.

Behemoths, in and out of the political arena, fell victim.

couple of old-time hunter friends; on Friday, a few politicians; on Saturday, some brother historians and authors. Between times he would seek relaxation by chopping down a few trees, swimming across Long Island Sound, taking ten-mile Marathons, and doing other things of a similar restful sort. No President ever worked so hard turning out material for cartoons.

In November of 1902, wearying of the monotony of Washington, the President went bear hunting down in Mississippi, pursued by hundreds of alert correspondents who gave us bulletins fresh every hour, and incidentally scared away all the bears. It must not be considered for an instant, however, that this period of activity was wasted. In the last analysis, this bear-hunting propensity of Mr. Roosevelt produced the crowning triumph of his personal popularity. From it evolved the "Teddy Bear," a household idol that threatened the very existence of the doll-baby and became a necessity in every house that had an active cradle.

By 1903, the President had become the great Mecca for sight-seers in Washington. He received such generous press notices that no tour of the Capital was complete without him. Congressmen were kept busy piloting curious constituents to the White House, and excursionists arriving in the Capital put off Mount Vernon and the Monument until the next day. Admiring fellow-countrymen brought all sorts of presents in token of their esteem: alligators from the South, hunting dogs from the plains, turkeys from New England, and bear cubs from the West. The state dining-room of the White House partook of the character of a zoo.

On his many flying trips throughout the land he was hailed as the Advance Agent of Posterity, a delicate compliment paid him by the Society for the Prevention of Race Suicide. In grateful appreciation he showed his gratitude by presenting a one-hundred-dollar check to a child that was named after him, and the next day hundreds of parents of all colors and races renamed their youngest children and sent special delivery letters to the eminent patronymic. Human touches of this sort have contributed immensely to Roosevelt's value as a provoker of cartoons.

His value in this respect is also greatly due to his courage in disregarding antiquated precedents. The fact that no other President had ever done a certain thing in no way restrained him. He revised all precedents to suit his own convenience. Time-honored traditions, unless strongly backed up by good reasons of a modern nature, were swept aside without a moment's hesitation. His trip to Panama, his illustrated message to Congress, his luncheon with Booker Washington, his one-hundred-mile horseback ride in seventeen hours, his trip in a submarine, his Brownsville flight, his boxing lessons, his jiu-jitsu instructions, his around-the-world battleship cruise, many of his messages directed at individuals—all of these activities are evidences of his disregard of old-fashioned notions of Presidential dignity.

No President has ever been in personal touch with as many sections of the country or as many classes of people as Mr. Roosevelt. His luncheons at the White House were attended by representatives of all kinds of men—those prominent in the labor world, the religious world, the financial, social, political, diplomatic and sporting worlds, and very frequently

A king deposed by a president.

all at one luncheon. With no false ideas about exclusiveness, he found time to talk with anybody who represented a new phase of life, and, in consequence of this wide familiarity with people and conditions, he has known how to reach the ear and favor of the country. In this respect he has had a great advantage over those statesmen who travel in a small circle of society, sit in a club, and try to imagine what is good for the people at large.

The year 1904 was a year of boundless possibilities, and the cartoons of that period record that Mr. Roosevelt embraced every one of them. The Presidential campaign, the St. Louis fair, and the Japanese-Russian war all provided settings in which our tireless Executive shone in original or reflected glory. Immediately after his election we find his annual message full of tariff revision, and a little bit later his struggles with a do-nothing Congress occupy the public attention.

The early days of 1905 were busy ones, both for the President and the cartoonist. In a single day when he was feeling particularly fit, the President straightened out the San Domingo difficulty, jumped on to Castro, sent a hot message to the Senate, dashed off an essay on the Race Question, handed the Standard Oil Company a hard jolt, made plans for a hunting trip, superintended the plans and preparations for inauguration, and then attended a banquet in New York.

The years of 1906, 1907 and 1908 are a bewildering succession of dramatic moves by the President.

Added to his wonderful energy in creating topics for discussion, there arose other conditions which equally provoked the cartoonist to activity. The country began to talk about a third term for the President or some occupation for him to follow after leaving the White House. They appointed him Prexy of Harvard, a member of The Hague Tribunal, a Senator from New York, and many other things.

He, not to be outdone, first got the Jamestown Exposition started, and then began the merciless war on stock juggling and manipulation that culminated in the panic of 1907. This was followed by a bear hunt in Louisiana, a waterway convention on the Mississippi, the dispatch of the battleship fleet, the elimination of "In God We Trust" from our gold coins, the installation of doctors in command of our hospital ships, a fierce war with a do-nothing Congress, a conservation conference, an African lion hunt, a row in the Navy, a denunciation of libelous newspapers, and the election of Mr. Taft, which constitute only a few of the achievements that have made great ammunition for cartoonists.

A complete list would be too long to include here, but those that are given will convince any one that Mr. Roosevelt has been a cornucopia of suggestions for the cartoonists and newspaper makers. It will be much harder work thinking up ideas now that he has retired from the fierce limelight of the capital city. (1909)

Teddy Roosevelt, jack-of-all trades and master of many.

Publicity for the Trusts

An EDITORIAL

Many will remember the article on Monopolies written for *The Saturday Evening Post* by Honorable Thomas B. Reed, which attracted wide attention at the time of its publication, nearly two years ago. In it he reviewed the situation and declared the feasible remedy for the checking of the growth of the trust evil to be publicity. The suggestion was taken up and generally approved. It seemed inadequate to the solution of such a big problem, but it was at least something that could be done. We see President Roosevelt urging the same point in his annual message, and it is almost impossible, now, to find an article upon the question which does not agree that the making public of the business of the huge combinations is the first essential to safety and sound financiering. Without it the people's interests cannot be protected.

As a result of the recent craze of trust forming, the mounting up of capitalizations until they rose to stupendous totals, it was inevitable that there should be many breaks and collapses. And so we have had them in plenty. A copper trust asked the public for $75,000,000 and got it, without showing why it should have it or what it did with it, and when the break began millions of values disappeared as if by magic. A falling market simply wiped out enormous wealth. Some of the other trusts faded from millions to thousands and then failed utterly. In all these cases the losses fell most heavily upon those who had been misled. They did not know what they were buying; they did not know what was done with their investments, and their only knowledge as to the whereabouts of their money is that it is gone. Publicity might not have saved all these credulous speculators, but it would have made the trusts more careful and would have curbed their amazing audacities.

Time only will show whether a good trust is productive of good to the people. But there is no doubt about the sentiment of the American people: they not only distrust but they fear vast accumulations of money in the hands of the few: there is a deep and widespread feeling that the great trusts which control so much of our trade and wield such vast power in public affairs should be compelled to make full statements of their operations and of their accumulations to the public on which they feed and from which they receive the authority for their existence. (1902) 🖝

The trust personified, circa 1907: a pirate standing guard over the ill-gotten gains made at the public's expense. Revolt was imminent.

HARRY B LACHMAN 07

Visiting the Twentieth-Century Bank

By IVY LEE

The man of small means who wanders through the ponderous labyrinth of wholesale banks along Wall Street feeling that there are "banks, banks everywhere, but not a bank to bank in," finds it all very different when he enters one of the uptown banking institutions, whose hands are ever seeking the small depositor. He will find, for example, that

there are two sets of clerks, one to handle the accounts of men and another to care for those of women. Opening from the aisle set apart for men is a men's writing and reading-room, supplied with desks, writing materials, lounging chairs, financial periodicals, a telephone, and other conveniences.

If the depositor is a woman she will find an even more cordial welcome awaiting her. In the Fifth Avenue Bank's reception room for women there is every possible luxury. Lace curtains, mahogany furniture, pictures, potted plants and books give an air of comfort and an attentive maid is always at hand. That women may not be oppressed by the formidable appearance of the bars and chilled steel of the safe-deposit room in the basement below, potted palms and pictures are placed here and there. In this department there are also rooms where the users of the strong boxes may be assured of absolute privacy and security. In yet larger rooms members of families may confer over the disposition of the securities of an estate.

One trust company maintains a ladies' department for its depositors in which only new banknotes and freshly coined gold and silver are paid out to its customers. In the cozy reception-rooms of this institution women customers are also invited to rest from their shopping or to come and meet their acquaintances or transact business of any kind. This company likewise offers its customers its advice upon any personal or legal point connected with the investment or disposition of funds—service for which a considerable sum of money might have to be paid in Wall Street. It is entirely true, as one of these institutions advertises, that it "treats its clients as guests."

Ideal banking conditions will not be reached until every man and woman with an income carries an account. The modern savings bank is distinctively the enemy of the old-fashioned hoarding stocking. All modern banking, from the savings institutions to the great wholesale banks of Wall Street, is intensely progressive. Its possibilities are not to be calculated. No ability however high, no brains of however superior quality, are more than it demands. The American Bankers' Association is spending $10,000 a year purely to assist in the education and training of bank clerks. The demand is for men of the highest possible type. To such individuals twentieth-century banking offers opportunities of exceeding honor, vast profit and illimitable power. (1904)

Where the Money Came From--
Carnegie, Master Artisan

By ARTHUR E. McFARLANE

The rich men whose names are in every one's mouth as synonymous for wealth and power, are an anxious, harrassed, miserable crew. Not one of them is happy. For he knows not in what hour he may tread upon the mines laid by his rival multi-millionaires and be blown to atoms. (1905)

A ndrew Carnegie was born in Dunfermline, Scotland, in 1837, and he was born into that radical hand-worker stock which had already begun to read and think for itself—but which was as yet wholly the downtrodden and unconsidered in the land. Although, however, his uncle had been flung into jail for preaching the rights of man, and his father had barely escaped the same fate, one of the first things that impressed small Andy was that those elders took it for granted that their ideas were very much more powerful than the bayonets which at the time seemed able to put them down.

The lad was given to know that the latter only looked powerful, and if a few score men merely studied and thought and labored hard enough, in a very few years they would have all those bayonets serving them, or could send them about their silly business, for that matter. It was a strange teaching for one so young and one to put fire in the small, impressionable soul.

But little Andy had no opportunity to see the proving of it in the kingdom of Great Britain; for in 1848 the fam-

The noble ideals of his Scottish kinsmen inspired the young Carnegie.

ily picked up its belongings and crossed over to America. The immediate cause of that emigration was the sudden prospect of the stoppage of work.

Taught by his mother, Andy had begun eagerly to read, which was as near as ever he got to the school-desk education. And now he went to work also, in a bobbin factory. He was paid $1.20 a week. The boy soon passed into the employment of the Pennsylvania Railroad. He moved from position to position, always with new varieties of the individual under him, new problems to handle.

It was now only a matter of into what particular work the young giant was to direct his conquering energies. It might have been railroad developing for himself, lumbering, iron or coal mining. As a matter of fact, it was almost all of these in time. But our feet take the nearest stepping-stone. The Pennsylvania had shown its intention to substitute iron for wood in its bridges. Into the Keystone Bridge Company, of Pittsburg, went Carnegie, borrowing most of the capital for this successful investment.

The story of the next thirty years was a foregone conclusion. There had been put into his hands smelting-works and rolling-mills; within his reach were any number of young men who knew how to do the things he only knew he wanted done; behind him was the mineral wealth of America.

He bought hundreds of square miles of ore and coal and limestone properties in Pennsylvania; he acquired his own natural-gas territory and piping; he had his own telegraph lines and railway connections; and when the mineral riches of upper Michigan began to be laid bare, his large hand swiftly descended and covered the Mesabi. To draw from it, he built ore docks and launched a fleet of carriers. To make the system complete, he added thereto one hundred and eighty miles of railroad and called Pittsburg a Lake Erie port. And always he was covering more hundreds of acres with his smelters.

The last and greatest was built upon the slag poured out as waste by the furnaces that had preceded it. Not only at Pittsburg, but up the river at Braddock and Homestead, at Duquesne and Beaver Falls and Conneaut, he had mills, each doing its specialized work and each unrivaled in its capacity for that work. Together they were a forge from which one could order the structural steel for a score of huge new office buildings, for a bridge across the Mississippi, for a fleet of battleships, for twenty miles of tubular "underground." In short, the man had made himself the Vulcan of the American mythology.

Yet this is mere immensity; it cannot give us the inner significance of the thing. We are ready enough to stand and ponder before the quarries which furnished the stone for Karnak and the Pyramids. Yet, for our modern time, those *ore* quarries of Pennsylvania and Michigan have constructed works of infinitely greater import. In the history of all countries there has been an epoch when there was a laying of material foundations.

For America that time is the present, and its foundations are not being laid in granite but in steel. It would be hard to measure how much nearer we have been brought to the moral and intellectual structure to be reared thereon by the swift immensity of this fundamental forge-building.

Carnegie's work repaid him not only in the gold of the spirit but in the hard metal of the mart. He amassed a fortune of two hundred millions.

We find him giving four millions for a pension fund for his aged and disabled employees, and other millions for institutes in which the children of those employees may equip themselves with the most invaluable of technical educations. He established picture galleries and concert halls, and calls for more public playgrounds and swimming baths. And if he has given little to churches, more than three hundred organs bear witness to his belief that music may deliver the message when the sermon fails. Whatever town may desire a library may have it for the asking.

He did much, too, by establishing the sliding scale, that first step toward actual cooperation between labor and capital. And he felt that "we have too long hours of labor in America. There is not a blast furnace or manufactory that has to run night and day at which the workers do not work twelve hours a day, the twenty-four hours being divided into two shifts. But to reduce the hours of labor in works that have to run night and day is something that can be done only by a general law compelling all such works to adopt eight-hour shifts." This was written after he had made a two years' attempt to establish eight-hour shifts at Pittsburg. Only one other rival firm followed his example, and by the hard law of competition the experiment had to be abandoned. (1904) 🐚

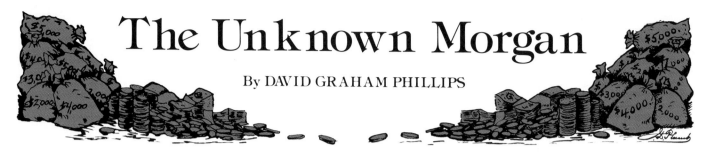

The Unknown Morgan

By DAVID GRAHAM PHILLIPS

He manages to hold control indefinitely of the properties he organizes, because the men who hold the large blocks of stock will do as he says; they rely on the soundness of his judgment, and they fear to oppose him. Morgan has the faculty of beating down an opponent by sheer animal force. He goes at his man as John L. Sullivan used to go at his—brutally straight. (1902)

It was one of the crucial days in the birth of the Steel Trust. Mr. Morgan's anteroom was filling with a distinguished company. Large properties were to be consolidated, and their multimillionaire controllers were to be placated, reassured, satisfied.

As the moments passed the anteroom filled, every man in it except Mr. Morgan's agitated messenger representing something important in this commercial world of ours. These great men were shifting impatiently, were talking sullenly or angrily in low tones, were acting as if they were "cooling their heels" in the anteroom of a king and did not in the least fancy being thus lowered from the estate and consideration to which they felt entitled.

American financier John Pierpont Morgan, far right, takes stock of Wall Street activities in a whimsical 1903 Post *drawing.*

DRAWN BY F. V. WILSON

And they were busy men, too, with no time to waste. Yet their time was wasting, and although their glances, concentrated under frowning brows upon the door of Mr. Morgan's office, seemed potent enough to hurl it from its hinges, it remained closed.

At last, after they had waited two hours and eleven minutes and a half, the door reluctantly opened. In the doorway appeared—a woman!

Who was she? A poor old woman who had about $20,000 on deposit with him—all she had in the world. It had been about $2,000, and, by investing it as Morgan can invest, he had multiplied it by ten. Then he had written her the good news in a formal way through the regular channels. And she had come down partly to thank him, chiefly to put him on the witness stand and satisfy herself that he was not gambling with her fortune. In all that time not by look or word or gesture had he shown her what she was doing—that she was wasting time than which there was none more valuable to more people anywhere on earth at that part of that day.

Another day we find Mr. Morgan at the house of a

young married couple who are his very near relatives. Only the servants welcome him—the young woman and her husband happen to be away. Mr. Morgan goes in and up the stairs to a bedroom.

In a little bed lies a baby, a near relative of Mr. Morgan's, as near as a grandchild. It recognizes the grandest, most sympathetic, most resourceful, most patient playmate it has discovered on earth thus far. And with wild gurgles of joy and wavings of rosy fists it makes for his mustache, his hair, his necktie, his dignity. Suffice it to say that Mr. Morgan drops sixty odd years off his life for about an hour.

Mr. Morgan is a good judge of stocks, of railroads, of individuals, of properties of all kinds. He is a good judge of paintings and china and sundry antiquities in tapestry, furniture and manuscripts. He is a good judge of men, no worse judge of women than the average man—perhaps a little better judge of them than the average woman. But to find his judgment at its best you must explore his views on babies. You wouldn't think it to look in his eyes or at his huge brow or cowcatcher-like jaw when he is at the reins recovering control of a runaway stock market; but any baby who is well acquainted with him or any mother who has seen him with her baby will tell you so. And it may not be amiss here to set down an opinion: No strong bad man ever played an hour, or half an hour, or more than a Napoleon's four or five minutes, with a baby. Weak bad men may have done it, but no *strong* one. The masculine heart that can harbor malignance cannot wash itself clean enough to fit its owner for an hour as playmate of a baby.

Not long ago a man was invited to spend a few days on the *Corsair.* She was lying off a harbor in New England when he joined her. He had been in-

dulging in splendid speculations as to the kind of sumptuous reveling time he would have provided for him. When he went aboard and inquired for his host one of the men said: "You'll find him in the galley." To the galley he went, and there was the presiding genius of international finance, clad in chef's white cap and apron and false sleeves—manufacturing a kind of pancake just then well thought of—no man has long to think well of any kind of pancakes or, for that matter, of pancakes in general. And after dinner everyone gathered about a big organ which Mr. Morgan has had built directly into the wall of the saloon, and sang—hymns! It may be proper to say that not even Mr. Rockefeller or Mr. Sage is more religious than Mr. Morgan.

In one respect, Mr. Morgan is a miser: he is a greedy, grasping, fierce miser of his business time. No man lives who has lifted himself so much as a hair's breadth above others that has not come to sympathize with any downpour of wrath upon time-wasters. And when a man rises to Mr. Morgan's height in affairs, when he has an important interest clamoring for every second of his time, for every grain of his brain-power, the time-waster becomes the chief plague of his life.

It is believed that he has recently made up his mind to put by no more money, but to spend all he makes—to spend it upon art collections and hospitals and other educational and philanthropic enterprises, public or semi-public. Certain it is that he had been careless of his own money-making opportunities.

With a largeness that bespeaks superior intellect and inferior appetites, and that rebukes the crawling covetousness of wealth for wealth's sake, he left the bulk of the quarry to his fellow-huntsmen, reserving only enough to maintain for him wholesome and necessary security, respect and dread. (1903)

Industry's Levy on Life

By WALDEMAR KAEMPFFERT

If fighting were as deadly as making phosphorous matches, riding in a locomotive cab, or riveting a girder in a truss two hundred feet in the air, swords would be beaten into plowshares and war abolished. How harmless soldiering is compared with the less picturesque vocations of peace.

One man out of every hundred and fifty is marked to lose an arm or a leg, to sustain a greater or lesser injury, or to die. A wage-earner toils constantly in the shadow of death. Every two days we kill more workmen than our troops lost in battle during the war with Spain. In New York City alone about 3,500 people, variously employed, come to a violent end every year—more than nine a day. Our industrial system as at present conducted sends a man every minute to the undertaker or the surgeon. Massacre annually every inhabitant in a city the size of Seattle, Paterson, New Haven or Albany, and you have the equivalent of the 100,000 violent deaths, which, on the basis of statistics collected by the Bureau of the Census for 1906, occur each year.

What becomes of the cripples, injured in their occupations, who are no longer able to earn a living? One study showed that for temporary injuries the settlements were usually fair, full wages being paid during the period of disability in many cases, generally by liability companies. When more serious harm was sustained, the following incongruous settlements were discovered: Spine injured, $20 and doctor; legs broken, $300; leg amputated, $100; fingers amputated, $50 to $150; death, $50 to $500, or funeral expenses; three ribs broken, $20; paralysis, $12; brain affected, $60; crushed foot, $50.

Fortunately, this sordid picture has another aspect. Some of the larger manufacturing companies, more philanthropically inclined than others, have devised systems of self-insurance. In one company, immediate medical attendance is given when injury or sickness occurs, and half-time wages allowed. For the permanent disability, an income for life is paid.

If a manufacturer can charge to the cost of production the wear and tear on apparatus, why should he not also charge for the wear and tear on his employees? Instead of casting a crippled factory hand out of his mill and leaving him to the care of the community at large, the cost of his disability or death ought to be paid for in the price of the product made by his hands. Something like this will ultimately take place, and with it an enormous expansion of the business of insurance.

Disease contracted in an occupation probably wreaks as much havoc as does cutting machinery. Not even a rash guess at the mortality can be ventured, so meagre is the information available. Letters sent to all the Unions comprising the American Federation of Labor brought forth responses that display no lively interest in bettering the environment of workers, although in many replies it was stated that conditions were often horrible. (1908)

The Moral Awakening

By WILLIAM JENNINGS BRYAN

For a generation the American people have been money-mad, and the quality of life has been measured by accumulations. The poor have imitated the rich, and the rich have created new records of extravagance. But the crisis is now past. From the press, the pulpit, the college, the Chautauqua platform and the home, is coming a healthy protest against the measuring of life by a pecuniary standard.

Assuming that the means employed in acquiring a fortune are legitimate, much depends on the spirit and purpose with which it is used. It is as selfish for a man of means to spend all of his fortune upon his family as it is to spend it upon himself, for the family is only a larger self. The country was shocked when Marshall Field ignored the claims of society and tied his tremendous estate up in a trust for the benefit of his family. That one could live in a world like ours, amid the appeals from worthy societies engaged in works of humanity, charity, education and religion, and still be deaf to the cries for aid and blind to the needs of the suffering and neglected, shows how small a heart this successful business man had.

When God gave us the earth with its fertile soil, the sunshine with its warmth and the showers with their moisture, He proclaimed, as clearly as if His voice had thundered from the clouds: Go, work, and your reward shall be proportionate to your diligence, intelligence and perseverance. That law has been reversed, and each decade shows a smaller and smaller percentage of the wealth remaining in the

hands of the wealth producer, and a larger and larger proportion making its way into the hands of the nonproducers. This condition is not only unnatural, it is dangerous. It is mainly due to man-made privileges and immunities—to law-made inequalities in distribution.

So great have these inequalities become that the President has sounded a note of warning. Protesting that these "swollen fortunes" should not be transmitted to posterity, he has suggested an inheritance tax to compel the predatory classes to disgorge at the grave.

There is a moral awakening that is world-wide in its extent; its effects are especially noticeable in this country, in the growth of altruism, in the increase in church activity, in the larger consideration given to sociological subjects and in the demand for a nearer approach to justice in government. The basis of this movement is the idea of brotherhood, and its purpose is not merely to stay each hand uplifted for another's injury, but to substitute in each the desire to benefit others in the place of the desire to over-reach. The means by which the movement is to be advanced is the cultivation of an ideal which will measure life, not by what one gets out of the world, but by what one contributes to the sum of human happiness.

The change in the ideal means a revolution in the life, whether the change takes place in the individual or in the group. An increasing number of our people realize that there is a higher end in life than the making of money. (1906)

Russia and Her Ruler-- The Czar

By W. T. STEAD

Russia is passing through a crisis which may result in anything, from a world-wide earthquake to a mere readjustment of her domestic arrangements. But the utmost that the most venturesome speculator will forecast is that whatever else will go under, the Czardom will survive. Not the old unlimited Czardom, for the present Czar has already self-limited his own autocracy, but still a Czardom of some kind will live on.

In the vast expanses of the Slavonian land, in the forests of the Northland or in the fertile steppes of the South, most villagers have no other conception of a government but that it is the expression of the will of the Czar. Even if the whole imperial family were blotted out in one fell swoop, the most advanced revolutionaries admit that, after a brief and abortive Republican experiment, the Czardom would come back via Caesarism. To the Russians a Czar is as indispensable as a queen-bee is to a hive. It may therefore not be inappropriate to begin a sketch of Russia and her ruler by an attempt to enable the reader to form some kind of an idea of the leading member of the imperial family.

Going back to his childhood, the family circle of Czar Nicholas II consisted of boys and girls who were not encouraged to grow up. Their father, Alexander III, liked them to be young as long as they could and the children heartily responded to **his wishes.**

The result was that both the pres-

Ill-suited for the demands of his destiny.

ent Czar and his brother Michael had next to no knowledge of the world and its ways at an age when most American boys feel they are free men of the universe. The natural craving of an over-worked autocrat—Alexander III died of overstrain—to keep his home as an oasis, free from questions of state which absorbed so many of his waking hours, led to the boys being kept boys at a time when they ought to have been men. The Emperor probably thought that there would be time enough for the lads to burden their young minds with affairs of state. He seemed likely to live for many years. But death overtook him when he was still in his prime, and Nicholas II found himself at the age of twenty-six called to occupy the most difficult throne in the world.

Never was mortal man less qualified to be an autocrat than the youth upon whom descended in all its crushing weight the well-nigh insupportable burden of the unlimited autocracy. He was of a loving, affectionate nature, full of generous aspirations, but absolutely without any experience of the rough workaday world. His boyhood passed in the midst of the pleasing illusion that the Czardom was not only the divinely appointed instrument for the salvation of the nation, but that the whole hundred millions of Russians were happily and enthusiastically conscious of the blessings vouchsafed them in the existence of the sovereign.

By nature full of a beautiful

idealism, dreaming as a boy of being "the people's king," like Scott's hero, James of Scotland, he suddenly found himself the responsible chief of a vast administration compelled to deal at every turn with the grim, stern facts of life. The strength of a Czar to control that administration lies in the confidence which he inspires in his people. But, under a plea of the need for protecting him against assassination, he was kept secluded from his subjects.

To be an unlimited autocrat with the limited strength of an ordinary mortal, to be supreme referee and final authority in every question that arises in the government of one hundred and forty millions of men, when you have only twenty-four hours a day in which to do it, is, on the face of it, impossible. But Fate compels him to attempt it, day after day, however much he may leave undone.

Nicholas II, in his struggles to get to the essence of his work, has dispensed with personal interviews, even with his own ministers. And under the same pressure he has dispensed with ceremony to such an extent that his ordinary daily life is as simple as that of any comfortable American citizen. Pomp and paraphernalia were conspicuously absent from the unpretentious little seaside villa where I last met the Emperor.

The dominant note of the Emperor's character is sympathetic receptivity, which, combined with good-hearted amiability, renders him at once one of the most delightful of companions, but one of the worst of disputants. His instinct is always to admit the force of whatever argument is addressed to him, his one thought is how to agree with his companion rather than to dissent from him, to see the good even in the worst of men and of things, and to avoid, if possible, the rough and craggy corners of angular dissent. With a philosophy not uncommon to mortals, he reconciled himself to his fate by a cheerful optimism which enabled him to see the best side of everything, even when it was most opposed to his own wishes.

Physically, the Emperor is a man somewhat below the middle height, being a little short in the legs. He has the bright blue eyes of the Dane, slight mustaches, light hair and a pleasant smile. He loves to smoke cigarettes and is fond of outdoor exercise.

There is at times a roguish twinkle in his eye, for

The Empress Alexandra Feodorovna remained his only human solace.

his sense of humor is keen and he is quick to see the humorous side of any subject. His manner is simple and unaffected; in conversation he is very quick and appreciative. He reads a great deal, is very quick to seize the salient point of what he reads, and has a retentive memory. Whatever may be his failings, they do not arise from lack of a keen interest in the world and its affairs.

Yet if I were to be asked wherein the Emperor's weak point lies I should say it is precisely in that he is not keen enough, not sufficiently close to the subjects with which he has to deal, to feel the full pull of his responsibility. You don't feel, somehow, as if he had a close, strong grip of things.

There is no doubt, of course, that the Emperor Nicholas has in the course of his reign tried various policies, abandoning a policy that has failed in order to adopt another that might have better promise of success. But history will probably blame him, not because he changed his policy so much as because he did not change it soon enough. (1905) 🪶.

Russia and Her Ruler-- The Revolutionary Usurpers

By W. T. STEAD

The speaker was a young man, short and wiry. He spoke in Russian: "A year ago in January I saw a hundred thousand workingmen parade quietly, without weapons or any means of violence, dressed in holiday clothes, accompanied by wives and children, going to petition the Czar. I saw these people lashed by mounted Cossacks and mowed down by rifle volleys—men, women, little children who could only scream their terror. I myself saw eight children clubbed to death. I decided to try [*sic*] if this Revolution dream could not be made practical. I joined the Revolutionists." (1906)

Russia has always been subject to the plague of revolutionary usurpers. Today, as in the previous centuries, success of the revolutionary usurper is possible only because of the widespread misery and discontent of the masses of the people.

It is in the country among the peasants that the revolutionary

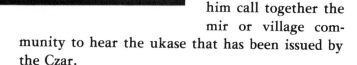

DRAWN BY EDWARD PENFIELD

usurper has ever achieved his most disastrous successes. For the method of the Revolutionist is to incite the peasant to burn, to steal and to slay by telling him lies in the usurped names of the Czar. In the eyes of the Revolutionist, the end justifies the means. But to the onlooker it is difficult to conceive more hideous cruelty achieved by more detestable means.

The Russian peasant is a simple, ignorant fellow, who with all his simplicity and ignorance holds fast to two fundamental ideas. The first is that no one ought to have more land than he can till, and the second is that the Czar is the Vice-gerent of Almighty God. The peasants are wretchedly poor. They have been taxed to the bone, and this year more than a dozen governments in the granary of Europe are in the grip of a terrible famine. They have been profoundly shaken by the disasters of the war.

Thus a deep, vague, but tormenting moral doubt has seized the peasant at the same time that his crops have failed and his children are dying of famine typhus. Just at this psychological moment a sudden excitement breaks out in his village. A great general in gorgeous uniform, accompanied by two or three other men in uniform, summons the starosta and bids him call together the mir or village community to hear the ukase that has been issued by the Czar.

The great and mighty Czar, the villagers are told, has decreed that all of the lands and goods of the landowners are henceforth to be made over to the peasants, and, further, on the following morning at eight o'clock the peasants must assemble with carts and horses at the neighboring estate of Prince A.B., and assist the peasants from the other villages in removing the goods, farm stuff, farm stock and other possessions of the landowner in order that

Thousands of men, women and children joined to air grievances before the Czar. Many—men, women and children—died at the hands of the Cossacks.

they may be divided among themselves. "And," continues the pseudo-general, "it is the Czar's will that you shall burn the prince's house and all the farm buildings to the ground. Only when you pull down the nests the crows will fly away."

The usual plan of operations is for the marauding peasants—each in his simple heart exultant that the Czar has at last given the land to his people—to approach the landowner's house and demand his keys. They say that the Czar has given everything to them, and that if the keys are given over they will not maltreat anybody. If, however, he refuses, they will be obliged to kill him and burn his house over his head.

But, it may be asked, can the landowner not rely upon his own peasants? If he does, he relies upon a broken reed. His own peasants will never begin the pillage. They stand aloof, watching curiously the colloquy between their master and the strange peasants who come in the name of the Czar to take the land. Undecided, anxious, torn by conflicting feelings of devotion to their landlord and their inbred longing for the land, they wait until the parley is over and the pillage has begun. Then, as they see strangers carrying off the sheaves that they have reaped, and staggering under the weight of furniture with which they have been familiar from childhood, a confused murmur breaks out: "We have more right to it than these fellows!" And in another moment your peasants have joined the pillagers and are looting with the best.

The next day the estate is skinned to the bone. The live stock are often butchered on the spot. Everything that is portable is removed. Then, as a climax, the torch is applied to the buildings and the ruined proprietor is soon left with his children to warm himself by the flames of his ancestral home.

That is the Revolution in Russia—the real Revolution which hides its grim and blood-red features behind no end of pretty masks of pleas for freedom and justice. There is no personal animus against the landed proprietors. In all the cases of agrarian outrage reported, I do not remember to have seen one in which the action of the peasants was excused or defended on the ground that they had legitimate grievances against the landlord. In many cases the peasants expressed and apparently felt the greatest regret that they had to plunder the property of one who had been their best friend. In the case of Prince Dolgoroukoff's estate, the whole proceeds of which were every year devoted to the upkeep of no fewer than seventy-four schools for the children of the peasants, the peasants wrecked everything, weeping as they plundered: "We wept, Little Father, we wept bitterly when we were doing it, for it went terribly against the grain, but we could not help it. We were told to do it, and so we did." (1905) 🐝

Imposing, intimidating and undeniably persuasive.

Ditch-Digging
in Panama

By SAMUEL G. BLYTHE

Sixty-nine steam shovels and more than thirty thousand men from all parts of the world are ripping a hole across the Isthmus of Panama, where, in a few years, there will be a waterway from the Atlantic to the Pacific wide enough and deep enough for any ship that wants to use it. The date set for completion is January 1, 1915, and it will probably be completed by that time.

The old French canal was of little consequence, and the old French machinery was found to be largely useless. The steam shovel is the instrument that makes that date seem reasonably certain. They are stretched all along the line of work, and they are tearing great holes in the dirt and rock, loading cars so rapidly it is hard to keep count, and insatiably eating their way down to the lowest levels. The best steam-shovel men in the world are on the job, so the head of the Steam Shovelers' Union has said.

Surveyors and sightseers mean history's in the making.

There is a tremendous rivalry among the steam-shovel men, artistically fostered by Secretary Joseph B. Bishop in the *Canal Record*, the weekly paper published on the Isthmus for the information of the employees and the outside world. Records are established every week.

Between five and six thousand Americans are employed on the Canal Zone. Many of them have their wives and children with them; so the total Ameri-

can population of that ten-mile-wide strip that runs across from Cristobal to Ancon is probably about ten thousand. In addition there are twenty-five or thirty thousand laborers from all parts of the world, many of these with wives, also, all living in Panama and making a marvelous human machine.

Many of the houses—low, wide-porched, airy and fitted for the tropics—were left by the French. They are screened from top to bottom, provided with electric lights, bathrooms and all sanitary appliances, and are very comfortable. The quarters an employee occupies depend on his rank on the pay-roll. Ordinary married quarters are four good-sized rooms, and the bachelors are given sitting-rooms and bedrooms, but two, at least, are required to occupy each set of rooms.

The main commissary is at Cristobal. It looks like a department store, and has as large a stock as many a pretentious place in the United States. The commissary usually has what is wanted, though fresh eggs are still a luxury, and the table can be kept from getting monotonous. There are one or two delicious native fishes, for instance. Supplies are furnished to the employees at cost, the quarters being provided free. Coupon books are issued and used by the employees, but no outsider can buy at these stores. Medicine and hospital attendance are free.

DRAWN BY EMLEN MC CONNELL

Health conditions, fortunately, are getting more satisfactory month by month. Both Panama City and Colon were yellow-fever ports, being constantly plague-ridden. They have been paved, sewered, and put in general sanitary condition. There has been no yellow fever since 1906, and no plague since 1905.

The main diseases are dysentery and malaria, and doctors are now getting the better of the latter. The rain-barrels and cisterns which were the breeding-places of mosquitoes have been abolished.

Except for the rainy season, when things are humid and sticky to a most irritating degree, life is much the same as in America. Americans have settled down to about the same sort of social and official relations that exist in Washington. If there is a big dance at the Tivoli, people from all along the line go over. If there is a minstrel show at Culebra there are visitors from all populated points. When there is a ball game they all flock in.

Organized activities in the Zone now abound. There are social and chess and various other kinds of clubs by the score. Four club-houses, built at an expense of approximately thirty-five thousand dollars each, feature billiard and pool tables, bowling alleys, gymnasiums, reading and card rooms and a lecture hall in each. The papers and magazines from the United States are plentifully supplied, and each club-house has a library of six hundred books. In addition, two amateur papers are published by the canal employees themselves.

Lecturers and small concert companies are brought to the Zone. The young men give entertainments of their own, principally minstrel shows. And now they have several fine baseball parks, well equipped, with a Zone league that plays during the dry season.

Nearly every afternoon the ladies of Ancon and

their friends who are in from along the line come in for afternoon tea. They have their dinners and their receptions and their bridge-whist parties, and there is a federation of women's clubs with twenty or more flourishing organizations in it.

All in all, the machine is now running like clockwork. Difficulties that seemed insuperable have been smoothed out. There is grumbling, of course, and a certain amount of discontent but, as a whole, the Americans are satisfied, for they have found that the life can be made pleasant, and the mere connection with such a wonderful work is a good deal of reward in itself for the disadvantages that must be endured. (1908) 🍒

Many a bashful suitor forgot his shyness as romance blossomed under the tropical moon.

The Great Race to the North Pole

From THE SIDELINES

Plans and Preparations

By HERBERT L. BRIDGMAN

Some half dozen nations are sending off Polar expeditions this year, and German shipbuilders at Wilhelmshaven are even constructing a submarine boat for Polar research. The United States, too, is eagerly searching for the North Pole. Lieutenant Peary, for example, is somewhere among the ice fields, with his wife following in search of him, and other seekers going after the wife. Among them all something of value certainly should be discovered. (1901)

We left Lieutenant Peary near Cape Sabine on Thursday, August 29. He was in splendid spirits and perfect physical condition. He had his party thoroughly in hand. He had behind him ten years' experience. Altogether the situation was such that we can safely predict that Mr. Peary will reach the North Pole within the year.

His outfit will include between sixty and seventy dogs, the backbone of any expedition that is to succeed. He already has one hundred tons of walrus cached for them and will add to his store materially before he starts.

There are many reasons why we feel confident that Lieutenant Peary will make a success of his expedition. In the first place, as I have said, he has ten years' experience behind him. Another factor that is going to have a strong bearing is Peary's superb mental and physical condition. The outdoor life that he has led in the bracing cold of the North has built up for him a system that was the envy of all of us who saw him.

Also, Peary is in thorough touch and sympathy with the natives, something no other white man has ever accomplished. He knows them like a book, and they know him and respect him thoroughly. In the opinion of all men who know anything about the subject nothing is more essential to success in reaching the Pole than the good will and cooperation of the natives. With this assured, half the battle is won. They are hardened to the climatic conditions, and, properly led, are fearless.

If all goes well we ought to be able to bring Mr. Peary back early next fall. (1901)

In the quest for the North Pole, probably no factor weighed more heavily in Robert Peary's favor than his friendship with the natives.

More than 60 dogs, heavy-coated and suited to Arctic climes, were part of Peary's well-laid plans.

CHARLES LIVINGSTON BULL

The Cook Controversy

By HENRY E. ROOD

Monday evening we on the *Roosevelt* [*Peary's ship*] made for Sydney, and at 7 a.m. Tuesday the *Sheelah*, with Peary's family on board, came bearing down upon us. An hour later Mrs. Peary and the children were in the Commander's cabin.

It was not until then, when a guest on the *Sheelah*, Colonel Borup of New York, came on board the *Roosevelt* and told us about it, that any of us on the Arctic ship had the faintest idea of the controversy raging between the partisans of Peary and the partisans of Doctor Cook. We knew in a general way, from brief bulletins by wireless at Battle Harbor, and from what had been said the previous Thursday by newspaper correspondents of the *Tyrian*, that some sort of a discussion was being carried on in the United States. But that it had reached the stage of bitter controversy, that any considerable part of the intelligent public was actually supporting Doctor Cook's claims to have beaten Peary to the Pole—which we knew were absolutely unsupportable to any degree whatever—was truly astounding news. We had not even suspected such a thing.

In his cabin, and while giving instructions for the day's work, and when he was sitting at the head of the officers' mess-table I had heard Peary say a dozen times, with his quiet smile: "Don't worry, gentlemen. We know which expedition reached the Pole and which one did not. Some day the whole world will know it." (1910) 🐾

World acclaim—fame and perhaps fortune—await the conquering hero. Behind the scenes an anxious family anticipates the moment of reunion.

The Discoverer of the Pole

An EDITORIAL

Finally, this Cook-Peary controversy is practically settled! The score is:

	COOK	PEARY
Columns of newspaper notice	17,869	9,453
Times portrait was published	1,387	783
Dinners	369	0
Cash receipts	$21,846	$3,427

Commander Peary is a good, deserving man, but it seems impossible that he should overcome this lead. Regretfully we consider him as good as beaten. His expedition was well planned and conducted with admirable ability. But in the final crucial dash to the front page, the grub and the box-office he played on a dead card: he got off on a blind lead and marooned himself, while his more fortunate competitor took possession of the goods.

Which of the two discovered the Pole, of course, is immaterial. It is generally conceded that several Scandinavians came to America long before Columbus; that an Italian, and not Henry Hudson, discovered the river which bears the latter's name. Probably the verdict of history will be that Swan Johnson, of Minneapolis, discovered the North Pole in 1914, while trying to find his way home from a Sons of Thor lodge meeting. (1909) 🐾

[History has decided in favor of Peary.]

JAMES PRESTON

The King on His Throne

By HARRISON RHODES

As the new century began, an English era abruptly ended with the death of Queen Victoria in 1901. After her 64-year reign, King Edward VII ascended the throne and ruled until his death in 1910.

———————

They say in London that His Majesty Edward VII is wearing out the throne by sitting on it. His love of pageantry and ceremonial is developing at a pace which is likely to render the lives of those immediately surrounding him a burden. He is never tired of presenting medals, welcoming em-

Perfection in manner and dress—required to pass the royal test.

bassies, and receiving delegations. If the British public is to pay for Royalty, Royalty is determined that the public shall have the worth of its money.

Behind the scenes, the King has a power of attention to detail which is as wonderful as it sometimes proves annoying to his household. Already the forthcoming Coronation is a topic of absorbing interest to the King, who keeps the Lord Chamberlain and his staff continually busy searching for precedents and rules. It has already been made known that the peers and peeresses will be expected to appear in brand new coronation robes which must be of red satin, ermine barred, and not merely of cloth. Real coronets are also to be worn, either gold or silver gilt, and the King has much to say as to the size and shape of all these glorious garments.

Meanwhile, he is not playing the hermit, and dines out somewhere almost every night of his life. He also has been playing "bridge" a great deal lately, and hostesses have had to arrange their parties with this game in view. Of course it is a great honor to have the King to dinner, but if notice that he is coming is given only the day before, as often happens, there is sometimes considerable trouble connected with the matter. The King, of course, invites himself, and sends a list of guests, and wherever the host, hostess and guests may be expected to dine the engagements must be broken.

One of the pleasures of having a King is that there is gossip about him, and stories of the King's kindness to ladies are innumerable. But one can rarely be sure of their strict authenticity. In the fierce glare that beats upon a throne, a smile from its occupant is construed as meaning volumes. And King Edward is publicly discreet. (1901)

New Developments

¶ *The world moves. We may not like it; usually we don't. But move it will, and the only certain thing about its movements is that what was yesterday, and what is to-day, will not be to-morrow. (1905)*

Looking Forward

By HARRISON RHODES

Shall women go into politics? An interesting question. *Will* women go into politics? is the practical question.

Fifty years ago debating clubs discussed, "Shall women go into business?" It was decided that they should not, yet women are swarming into business, and thinking out new lines of work. How long before the business woman demands the franchise? And, when she is numerous and determined, how is mere man to stand out against her? (1905)

I do not write this story from any love of writing. I write it to point a lesson and to sound a warning. I am an old-fashioned woman, and I glory in it. It has been my privilege to live through the best part of a century which must forever go down in history as the Golden Age of the race.

As a child I must have seen something of the Revolution. I can just vaguely remember my mother's departure to join Belmont in her great expedition, the march on Washington, which ended in the capture of the Capitol and the expulsion of the rebellious male Senate. She left the house just at twilight. I can see her now buckling on her sword, which made me think of a hatpin. She was fortunately a widow, and thus free to go to the front. She kissed us girls goodby. I can recall her words.

"Thank God," she exclaimed, "I have borne women-children! If anything happens to me you can carry on the fight!"

But these are memories of long ago, and I want to talk of conditions now. The Twentieth Century has been one of happiness and prosperity under the loving rule of Woman, seated at last on the throne.

Mattie Avery, the great historian of the Revolution, has crystallized our times in a phrase.

"In the Twentieth Century," she says in the *History of the Triumph of Woman*, "Man was put in his place, and still better, kept there!"

Happy, indeed, were those mid-century days! But now what do we see? Discontented men, unsexed creatures, not content with their work, with their place in the factory or at the plow, trying to be doctors, lawyers, politicians—women, in short. There is a "Man's Rights Movement," if you please, and I understand that there are members of my own sex so shameless and misguided as to lend it their support. This morning I was roused from my refreshing sleep by a rowdy procession going up Fifth Avenue carrying banners marked "Votes for Men!" It was headed by that Mackay boy, who might better be occupied remember-

ing that his great-grandmother fought and bled in the grand Revolution. We have no longer any pride of ancestry in this country!

I am not an unreasonable woman. I am ready and willing to understand masculine ambition, and to admit that there may be exceptional men whose minds would actually fit them to take part in what I may call the intellectual half of the world's work. But nothing could be more wrong than to encourage the ordinary man to attempt what is quite beyond his powers. The question was settled by God and Nature when man's body was made strong and his mind weak, while woman's mind was strong and her body weak. The hard, rough physical work of the world must be done by men. Are women to dig ditches, and scrub floors, and wield pots and kettles in the kitchen? No. This is all man's sphere. Woman's domain is the imagination, the intellect. She guides and controls man's ruder strength, and so she must to the end.

Senator and Mr. Morris

But this is not telling my story...

Every one knows or knows about Senator Effie Morris, of Rhode Island, and Mr. Morris, her husband. Mr. Morris was Frederick Challineur, of the New York family. I like the Challineurs, yet I should never have advised a serious-minded woman to choose a husband from that family.

I was at their wedding. Fred Challineur made a beautiful groom, and, old woman though I am, I did not regret my privilege of kissing him.

"There, Mr. Morris!" I said. "And I hope you're going to be very happy."

"I am, Aunt Mary," he said. "I'm so interested in Effie's political career. I want to understand it; I want to help her in it."

I am an old woman. I am a relative. I thought it was my privilege to speak bluntly.

"The best way for you, Fred, to help your wife in her career is to mind your own business. Stay in your garage, play your polo, but let politics alone."

It was Effie who answered me, not Fred. She drew herself up rather haughtily.

"I wish my husband to be interested in my work, Mrs. McCarnobie," she said. "I want Fred's help in my career."

"If you want Fred's help you'll probably get it," I answered, a little tartly. "But you'll probably need more help soon; mine, perhaps—at any rate a woman's—to get you out of the trouble your husband's help has got you into. You're a Man's Rights woman, are you?"

That stung her.

"Well, no, not exactly——" she began. I turned on my heel and walked away, little realizing how nearly true my prophecy was to come.

DRAWN BY WILL GREFE

They went at once to Washington to live. Very soon Fred and Effie started what was called "a political salon," and they got hold of all the queer fish in Washington. Fred was a devotee of all the new cults, an advocate of all the new reforms. Mind you, I don't scoff at men's power altogether. Often they can rouse public opinion, and by indirect influence, which is the natural, wholesome, manly way, can often induce women

Grafting was a respectable business—'til Wild Mag came along.

was to bring grafting into line with the other great industries of the country, to control it to the national advantage. Now, perhaps the most distinguishing feature of the early Twentieth Century was the growth of unions, and the complete triumph of the trades-union principle. What more natural then than a grafters' union, and the elimination of non-union grafters from the United States Senate? The reckless and extrav-

to take up a burning cause and do something about it. I was, for example, glad enough to see Fred organize an athletic carnival week or gymkana to raise funds for the Society for the Suppression of Male Infanticide in China. Of course, one sees the Chinese point of view. In a congested population naturally too many male infants are mere cumberers of the earth. Still, humanity is humanity, and I think it a generous and praiseworthy impulse on the part of American men to save the little Chinese boys; to remember that if there is the stern, logical Chinese mother there is as well the tenderhearted Chinese father who will miss his useless little boy as much as he would his splendid girl child. Such activities seem to me well within man's sphere.

Now, if our century has done any great work in what I might call the actual technic of politics, it is in systematizing and regularizing graft. Woman's task here

agant methods of securing legislation prevalent in an earlier day have long since disappeared. Corporations and individuals interested in passing or killing a certain bill make definite financial tenders to the Senate, not individual Senators or cliques. This is dignified, and moreover it is the most direct and definite way of ascertaining what the country's feeling on any subject is. *Vox populi, vox dei.* But that voice used to be hard to hear. Now it is definitely put before the Senate in intelligible sums. As one of the old philosophers observes, "Money talks." And whoever wants a bill passed badly will surely be willing to pay for it; otherwise one doubts his sincerity. Under the present system Senators know what they can count on. Broadly speaking, the country knows. Senators who vote for a bill share and share alike in what is paid for it, and the Senator who fails to distribute, in public charities and educational endowments in his state, about what other Senators do can easily be detected. The system is well oiled, easy-running. And the country is prosperous. Are we never to let well enough alone? Now comes Senator Margaret Clark of Wisconsin—Wild Mag of the West, as they call her—and begins a campaign in favor of the right of individual or non-union grafting.

Fred told me something of these new ideas at one of their "red flag" dinners, as I call them. Union grafting was paralyzing the Senate, he said. Individual action was nullified.

The trouble all began with that Baldwin-Mitchell Bill, in which Fred, as a philanthropic man, took such a violent interest. It was in itself an admirable measure, designed to safeguard young male immigrants. It was in essentials a non-partisan bill. The opposition was merely questioning the practicability and wisdom of certain of the bill's provisions. There was a small offer of graft from some of the steamship companies which didn't like the restrictions imposed, but it was popularly supposed that this was so small as to be negligible, and that the bill passed on its merits, or at any rate without the transfer of funds. "Wild Mag" was naturally strong for it and made an almost impassioned speech on high moral grounds in favor of it in the Senate. There was a general wish to conciliate on such easy terms a firebrand like her, when there was a good bill, and nothing important to be gained by not passing it. Effie Morris, for example, voted for it, and told me she did it mainly to please Fred.

"I meant to vote for it anyway," she said jokingly to me one afternoon at the club, "but I let him beg hard for it, and made him think that I was doing it all for him. Why not? There was nothing in it for me or for any one."

And so every one supposed till the *New York Hourly*—one edition each hour of the twenty-four—produced the documents in the case, and the scandal broke. By Friday morning at 7 o'clock, readers of the *Hourly* were gloating over the letter from "Mr. Senator" Morris to Wild Mag Clark.

"Dear Margaret," it began. I was grateful that it was no more intimate.

"I thank you for the check. Fifteen thousand dollars is a tidy sum. It will enable me to take my ponies to Newport for the polo this year. It's handsome of those bighearted, humanitarian men in New York to encourage individual freedom in legislation and grafting. Deprived of a voice in the government of their country though they are, they are yet struggling to help. Our bill has gone through, and it is pleasant to have the reward.

"I appreciate the compliment you pay me in sending the check to me rather than to my wife. Hers was the vote in the Senate, but she does not treat me in the old, misguided way, as an inferior, but as an equal, a counselor, a friend. In this matter she and I are acting together. We are one."

There was a little more, thanks to the Wisconsin Senator for having developed his intelligence, but was this not enough to compromise Effie hopelessly? I turned fairly cold as I read the headlines:

"Independent Grafting. Senator Clark withholds from colleagues money paid for passage of Baldwin-

Keeping informed, studying both sides of an issue—a top priority in decision-making.

Mitchell Bill. Shares only with small clique."

"Senator Effie Morris accused of Treachery to Party. Indignation in Washington and in Rhode Island. Rumors that she will be asked to resign."

" 'Unworthy traditions of Senate,' say Party Leaders."

And then snappier papers:

"Did Senator Morris know? Mr. Senator Morris' Letter to 'Dear Margaret.' Statement by Wild Mag."

And an hour later:

"Reported that Senator Effie repudiates her husband's authority to act for her. Said will sue for divorce."

The fat was indeed in the fire!

I shall never forget the midnight conference at my house. We had hoped to escape detection. But as we talked we could hear the reporters tapping on the roof, while the walls fairly sizzled as they tried to get through with X-rays to photograph us.

Fred was nervous, but looked very handsome in his agitation. He was dressed in black. There were, besides Effie, Clark and myself.

"First of all I want to say," began Effie, in a calm manner, "that I have every confidence in Fred's having been nothing more than foolish."

"You have my word of honor for that as well as his." It was Wild Mag who spoke. "I may not always have behaved toward the weaker sex as I should. But this time, Morris, I ran straight."

"I believe you," answered Effie. "And I have to acknowledge I did too."

"As to the difficulties this disclosure creates, I don't want you to think of me. The important thing is for you two to save your happiness."

"I'm not quite sure that you oughtn't to divorce him anyway, Effie," I said. "Very often a woman has to try three or four times before she gets a good husband."

"Oh, come off, Effie, old girl," said Fred. He spoke roughly, like the true man that at heart he is. He struck a match on—on his trousers and lit his pipe. But there was, I felt, an undercurrent of deep feeling in what he said. And his words should sink deep into the hearts of American men, of husbands wandering from the home. "I'll make it straight with the papers and the Senate. I'll be able to prove at least that you know nothing of what I was doing. Senator Clark here must look out for herself, as I'm sure she can. I'm going to give up your 'bally' politics anyway and stick to the ponies. Men can't understand politics, Effie; I see that now. Men are foolish to try to go out of their sphere. I can take you on at tennis, Ef, but not at legislation. So I'm through with it. I'm glad, if you'll take me back, to go back as an old-fashioned man, just a husband."

Are the words not beautiful, mellow with that old mid-century radiance? I confess my throat felt choky and my eyes wet as Fred held out his arms to Effie, who after a moment's pause was infolded in them.

Fred is now the President of the Men's Anti-Suffrage League, one of the most useful men in the community and one of the happiest husbands. He is content to accept Nature's mandate, and leave the intellectual work to women. (1910) ❧

Uncle Sam in the Scientific World

By RENÉ BACHE

Nearly twelve millions of dollars are spent annually by the United States Government on scientific investigations and in the application thereof to useful purposes. It seems an enormous sum, but there can be no question that it is invested far more profitably—looking at the matter from a purely practical standpoint—than any equivalent amount disbursed under appropriation by Congress for other objects.

The Patent Office, which cost $1,448,000 last year, is in reality a great scientific establishment. It is a congeries of thirty-eight scientific divisions, which together compose a bureau of the Interior Department. Into this bureau ideas from all over the country are poured indiscriminately, as into a hopper, by inventors, and, after being sorted out, they are referred for consideration to the divisions where they properly belong. The complexity of the machinery employed in this great mill for grinding out new and useful contrivances (the valueless ones being thrown aside) may be judged from the fact that electricity alone absorbs the attention of three of these divisions, one of which attends to telegraphs and telephones, the second to motive power and railroads, and the third to lighting, heating and signaling.

There are also three distinct chemistry divisions in the Patent Office—made necessary by the fact that so many arts and industries are based upon

Will Keith Kellogg formed the Toasted Corn Flake Company in 1906. To ensure its authenticity, W.K. put his signature on every box. Corn Flakes were the result of research for a bread substitute; and although he developed other products (Rice Krispies, All-Bran), he remained the "Cornflake King."

chemistry in one way or another. All preparations for bleaching and dyeing that are submitted, as well as new explosives, have to be carefully analyzed, and the composition of every medicine for which a patent is sought must be ascertained. To get a patent, a remedy must be a hitherto undiscovered laboratory product—not a mere prescription. However, within the space of a few lines it is impossible to give a comprehensive account of the work of this great bureau, the expenditure for which is more than balanced by its receipts, the surplus of profits turned into the Treasury last year being more than $194,000.

The annual appropriation for the Geological Survey is about $1,500,000. It is the business of this bureau to map the mineral-producing regions of the country and to study its water resources.

Incidentally, the Geological Survey is a bureau of discovery. Not long ago a party of its explorers in Alaska located a gold belt which may yet rival the deposits of South Africa—a strip of gold-bearing rocks at least 500 miles long, which is the source of the yellow metal found so richly in the placers of the Yukon Valley. This strip, which passes from British territory into our own domain near Forty-Mile Creek, crossing the Yukon not far from the mouth of the Porcupine River, runs through a range of low mountains, and on the higher levels, where the rocks are bare, the gold may be seen on the

Dr. Clark's prediction was accurate—although diamonds of gem quality have not yet been synthesized successfully. The Federal Trade Commission defines a "synthetic gem" as one whose chemical, physical and optical properties are identical to those of the mineral as it occurs in its natural form. A slightly modified version of the flame-fusion technique developed for producing synthetic rubies and sapphires in the 1900s by August Victor Lewis Ver Duil is still in use by the gem industry today.

surface in bright specks. There are gigantic bodies of ore in sight, which will be easily accessible when the region is opened up by a railroad.

When, a dozen years ago, a "fault," or break-off, in the deposit of gold and silver at Leadville was found, causing the owners of the mines to fear that the supply of precious metals from that source was on the point of exhaustion, one of the experts of the Survey made a study of the locality, and, discovering how the rocks of the earth's crust thereabout had slipped out of their original position, showed exactly where a continuation of the deposit ought to be struck if sought at a specified depth beneath the surface. The miners followed the directions given them, and behold! the seams filled with silver and gold again revealed themselves, resuming their interrupted course through the rock formations beyond the "fault."

A deposit of mineral rubber was found recently in Utah. The stuff is black, elastic, waterproof, and looks, feels and acts exactly like ordinary rubber.

Other discoveries were made by accident. Dr. David T. Day, examining, recently, in the San

Francisco Mint, some platinum-bearing sand from the extreme northwest of California, separated from it a pure alloy of iron and nickel—much the same metallic mixture that ordinary meteorites are made of. This led to finding a big deposit of nickel in the bed of the stream whence the sand came, in first-rate form for use in the new-fangled nickel storage-batteries.

George F. Kunz, the gem expert, who is connected with the Survey, heard, not long ago, of something new in the way of a precious stone that had been found near San Diego, California. He sent for a specimen, and discovered that it was a species of gem hitherto unknown, related to the emerald, very brilliant, and resembling a pinkish diamond. It is now coming on the market under the name of "Kunzite." Meanwhile, all of the important gems have been analyzed in the laboratory of the Geological Survey, whose chief chemist, Doctor Clark, is of the opinion that every one of them, even including the diamond and ruby, will be reproduced some day by artifice. All that is needed (their composition being exactly known) is apparatus working on a great scale, with a long allowance of time for the formation of the crystals.

For many years past the U.S. Navy Department has been making elaborate experiments with torpedoes, which are kept very secret, and recently the War Department has done a good deal of work with submarine mines, for the defense of our harbors. Officers of both services are constantly engaged in the study of "ballistics"—a branch of investigation that has to do with firing guns. At Indian Head,

HOOVER SUCTION SWEEPER
Electric

Spring cleaning is no easy task, but it would seem overwhelming without the aid of the vacuum cleaner. James Murray Spangler patented the first portable vacuum in 1908, modeled after the huge stationary machines used in big stores and office buildings. He combined a revolving brush with suction and called it the Electrical Vacuum Carpet Sweeper, William Henry Hoover bought the rights, and the cleaning revolution was off to a roaring start.

on the Potomac, the Navy maintains a chemical laboratory for experiments with explosives, and another laboratory, for similar purposes, is supported by the Army at Sandy Hook, New Jersey.

One great executive department, that of Agriculture, is wholly devoted to the pursuit of scientific investigations, its entire annual appropriation, nearly $6,000,000, being expended, directly or indirectly, for such purposes. It is, in fact, nothing more than a group of scientific bureaus, which make it their business to study every imaginable thing that is of interest or value to the farmers.

The work done by the Chemistry Bureau of this department is wonderfully varied and important. Within the last few months they have made twenty-five pure yeasts, derived from the natural fermentation of ciders in various parts of Europe and in this country. These they have grown by inoculating sterilized apple-juice with them, and it is found that, by their means, ciders of different kinds and flavors can be produced from the same juice. Soon, the yeasts in question will be made available to apple-growers, and it is expected that they will markedly improve the cider output of the United States.

In the Dairy Division much attention is paid to the study of microbes that ripen butter and cheese, giving to them their distinctive flavors. Such germs may now be purchased, put up in little bottles, and utilized for inoculating the milk from which the cheese or butter is to be made. Another recent discovery, which is said to be saving $5,000,000 a year in Wisconsin alone, is a method of treating the seeds of cereals, especially oats, by soaking them in a weak solution of formalin, to prevent "smut."

Now that so many tropical islands have been annexed by Uncle Sam, the economic plants of those latitudes have assumed a new importance from the viewpoint of our Government. But meanwhile efforts are being made to push other fruits and field crops northward by breeding frost-proof varieties. Already there has been obtained a hardy orange which is expected to

The disposable razor blade began a new phase of American life—the throwaway society. King Camp Gillette's brainstorm was not an immediate success. In 1903, only 51 razors and 168 blades were manufactured. By the end of the decade, over 13 million blades were being sold each year and Gillette had factories in four countries.

Gillette Safety Razor

defy the climate of all the Gulf States—a cross between the every-day sweet orange and a species from Japan.

The navel orange was originally introduced into this country by the Department of Agriculture in 1872, being fetched from Brazil. It is said to have added $60,000,000 to the taxable wealth of the state of California.

There is no branch of science to which the Government of the United States is not devoting attention. Washington is to-day the greatest scientific centre in the world, not even excepting Berlin or Paris. The best brains obtainable are employed by Uncle Sam in every branch of research, and upon the investigations they are pursuing and the discoveries they are making will be based to a very great extent the future welfare and prosperity of the country. (1905) 🍇

The navel orange is novel in one respect—no seeds! —a phenomena propagated by grafting. Today 40% of the crop is used in the production of orange juice; prior to 1920 the orange was regarded primarily as a dessert fruit.

High Flyers

By WALDEMAR KAEMPFFERT

An aeroplane may be defined as a surface propelled horizontally in such a manner that the resulting pressure of air from beneath prevents its falling. It is an aerial skate gliding on a medium more treacherous and less sustaining than the thinnest ice. To stay aloft it must skim the air so swiftly that it has no time to fall. Motion, incessant motion, is the secret of an aeroplane's flight. If it stops it must inevitably fall. The faster it glides the safer is the man whose hand grasps the controlling lever.

All aeroplanes are air skates. But these air skates may assume different forms. In a general way they may be divided into two classes —biplanes or double-decked machines and monoplanes or single-decked machines. The Wright, Curtiss and Farman machines are biplanes; the Bleriot and Latham machines are monoplanes. Why do Wright and Curtiss prefer the biplane, and Bleriot and Latham the monoplane, if both are alike in principle? Simply because each style has certain advantages over the other. The biplane has a larger supporting surface, which means greater carrying capacity; it can be handled almost as easily as if it had but a single surface; it is more easily controlled; and it is trussed and braced like a bridge so that it can be subjected to strains which might crush an ordinary monoplane. On the other hand, the monoplane is speedier than a biplane because, having but a single horizontal surface, it encounters less head-on resistance. Spreading but a single horizontal surface, as it does, it is difficult to make it stiff and strong.

The daring young man in the flying machine dreamed of the day he would court his beloved in the clouds.

Both monoplanes and biplanes have made remarkable records. Only a few weeks ago Santos-Dumont, in his wonderfully light and delicate Demoiselle—a monoplane costing only one thousand dollars—wrested from Curtiss the world's speed record by traveling at the rate of fifty-five miles an hour; while more recently still Santos-Dumont's record has been beaten by Orville Wright in his biplane. With Santos-Dumont on board the entire weight of the apparatus is only two hundred and sixty pounds, noteworthy when it is considered that many monoplanes weigh over half a ton with the pilot. So far as distance is concerned it seems that both monoplanes and biplanes, like automobiles, are limited only by the capacity of their gasoline tanks. At Rheims, Farman flew one hundred and twelve miles in three hours four minutes and fifty-six seconds and was obliged to stop only because of darkness. Although aviators prefer to skim near the ground at heights of fifty to one hundred feet, the aeroplane can ascend, theoretically, to any height. What can be done in this respect is shown by Orville Wright's recent performance in spirally reaching a height variously placed at fifteen hundred, sixteen hundred and seventeen hundred feet.

The monoplane or biplane pilot is confronted with the difficult problem of maintaining his equilibrium. That fragile, delicate mechanism of planes, rudders and propellers with which he rushes through the air is subjected to two forces—the pressure of the air and its own weight. The air pressure acts upward and, therefore, sustains the aeroplane in flight; the weight of the different parts naturally acts downward. If the center of air pressure or upwardly-acting force happens to shift to one side of the center of gravity the machine will capsize and crash to the ground. Why? Because the upwardly-acting pressure is more powerful at high speed than the downwardly-acting weight of the machine. The only way to maintain equilibrium is to bring the two forces together in the middle so that they will act, the one upward and the other downward, through the same point. When the aviator has accomplished this feat he has brought the center of air pressure and the center of gravity into coincidence. Since the wind, despite its apparent steadiness, is in reality composed of innumerable puffs and gusts, currents and counter-currents, the center of air pressure is constantly shifting, which renders balancing extremely difficult.

In order to bring the wandering center of air pressure back into coincidence with the center of gravity the Wright brothers have devised a method of warping or bending the outer ends of the planes. The same balancing effect is obtained by hinging flat surfaces or tips to the outer ends of the planes and swinging them up or down as the exigencies of the moment may require. In France these hinged tips are called *ailerons*. In the latest of Mr. Curtiss' machines these *ailerons* are removed entirely from the ends of the main planes and placed between them. Although changed in position their function remains the same.

Before it can fly, every monoplane and biplane must be in motion. Various forms of launching contrivances have been invented to impart this initial velocity. The late Professor Samuel P. Langley, to whom we are indebted for a wealth of aerodynamic information, used to place his models on a car which ran on a track and which fell down at the end of the rails, and thus released the model for its free flight. The Wright brothers likewise employ an inclined rail. When their machine has shot forward a sufficient distance and acquired headway it rises into the air. In order to overcome the objection of employing a track, Curtiss, Bleriot, Farman, and indeed almost all aviators with the exception of the Wrights, mount their aeroplanes on bicycle wheels. The machines run along the ground for perhaps a hundred yards and are then lifted into the air by the upward pressure on their slightly-tilted horizontal rudders.

A modern bicycle is a useless aggregation of wheels and sprockets until one has learned to ride it. Yet bicycling is mere child's play compared with flying. A bicycle rider is concerned chiefly with

keeping his side-to-side balance. An aviator must maintain not only his side-to-side balance, but his fore-and-aft balance as well, and that, moreover, at almost express-train speed. It is said that after Delagrange had covered about six miles in one of his earlier flights he was lifted from his machine in a state of utter exhaustion. Farman's first flight covered only a few yards. Six months later he flew two miles in a circle. Yet the machine which, after the first attempt, obstinately refused for two whole months to soar for more than a few yards at a time was precisely the same machine that later flew under more or less perfect control. After the pilot has acquired the requisite skill he seems capable of daring almost anything. Lefebvre amused the public at Rheims by performing acrobatic feats in the air on one of the lighter Wright machines and by taking an occasional flight across country.

The future of the aeroplane is not without possibilities. It is highly probable that it will become what the bicycle once was—a vehicle of sport. France has already set the pace. Perhaps in a few years our gilded youth will fly over our heads in aeroplanes instead of past our noses in automobiles.

Before that time, the aeroplane must become a reasonably safe machine. Some means must be contrived of balancing it automatically. Mechanical methods have been devised with this object in view, but these are presently unserviceable because they impose new burdens upon a machine which must be of feathery lightness. For the moment nothing practicable has been done in the way of designing aeroplanes which preserve their stability when driven slowly. Perhaps the inventor of the future may solve this very difficult problem. Stability, at present, depends upon the speed at which the machine is propelled. Although the Wright biplane travels at the rate of approximately forty miles an hour and Farman's Voisin biplane is credited with as much as forty-five miles an hour, still higher veloc-

ities are necessary if the machine of the future is to remain on an even keel without the exercise of that eternal vigilance on the part of the aviator which at present is the price of aeronautic safety. A distinguished English authority, E. W. Lanchester, has stated that an average speed of at least sixty miles an hour must be maintained in order that the machine may travel faster than those occasional gusts which to the aviator are as perilous as sunken rocks to a mariner. If a speed of one hundred miles an hour could be kept up an aeroplane could travel in any wind, and not, as at present, merely in a gentle breeze. The whole problem seems to be one of engines and propellers and, therefore, not beyond solution. When that solution comes the flying machine will be the master of the wind and not its slave. (1909)

Even its full-sized counterpart was considered little more than a toy, a "vehicle of sport," in 1909.

DRAWN BY
SARAH S. STILWELL WEBER

Farming with Power

By FORREST CRISSEY

It is not a wild prophecy to predict that within ten years power tractors will prevail in the level lands of the West in the ratio to teams that the automobile now bears to driving horses on the boulevards of the big cities. Today horseless farming has become so confirmed a fashion in the new country of the Dakotas and Montana that the development of that region, from the richest cattle and sheep range in America to a vast wheatfield, is being hastened by not less than ten years.

The power tractor, which can plow as much land in an hour as a team of five horses can turn in half a day, is not only for the big farmer who counts his holdings by sections; it is equally the salvation of the homesteader with his hundred and sixty or his three hundred and twenty acres—the man who has really settled on his land, who is there to found a home, and who needs to get the greatest possible return from his land right at the start in order to make both ends meet.

The rapidity with which horseless farming turns a frontier wilderness into a prosperous and civilized community is perhaps best illustrated by the changes that have taken place in the range country through which the latest transcontinental railroad line has been constructed. Four years ago it was a free cattle range and a plow was an object of curiosity and contempt. Then Scranton, North Dakota, was not on the map; today it is a humming town with one thousand inhabitants and two prosperous banks. The biggest part of its growth, so its business men affirm, is the result of horseless farming. About sunrise, any morning in the cropping season, this little town is alive with automobiles scooting out across the prairies to farmshacks that serve as day headquarters for the horseless farmer—who lives in a comfortable house in town.

According to the consensus of opinion in this town, big-power farming is the secret of this sudden and astonishing growth. Without horseless farming the present growth would undoubtedly not have been attained for a decade or more.

The present style of tractor, of the kerosene or gasoline type, has a road speed of about two and a quarter miles an hour, or about the walking speed of an ordinary team of draft-horses. Tractor manufacturers are coming to recognize the demand

The tractor has revolutionized farming, increasing yields and efficiency. The human result of all this has been to make farm work easier and farm hours shorter, both for men and for women. The lumpish stooping shoulders of the man with the hoe have given way to erect carriage and lithe stride.

for engines of higher speed on the road and also for engines of lighter construction than those generally in use. Very likely the time is near at hand when the smaller farmer of Illinois, Indiana and Ohio will be able to buy a smaller tractor, constructed to do the work of about fifteen horses and capable of being driven over ordinary roads at the trotting speed of a draft-team. This machine will undoubtedly be spring-mounted, of steel construction and of lighter weight than the prevailing type.

Economy in time, labor and operating cost is by no means the main argument in favor of the power machine as against the horse. Power farmers are quick to respond to this point with the statement that the tractor engine does its work so much more efficiently than does the horse team that the difference in crop results forces itself to the front as the big consideration.

Summer fallowing is the prevailing practice in most of the wheat sections of the Northwest. Its main purpose is to expose the ground to the action of the sun and air for the purpose of liberating plant food not available for nourishment of the crop with-

out that exposure. Every day that is allowed to elapse between the cutting of a field of grain and the turning under of its stubble is a period of riot for the weeds. This is a problem of extreme difficulty to the team farmer which is overcome with admirable ease by horseless-farming methods. After a reaper has cut one swath around the field it is mated with a six-bottom gang of plows and the tractor hauls them both around the field, the plows turning the soil on which stood the first swath of grain and the harvester cutting a second swath and dropping the bundles upon the freshly turned ground. With this combination the weeds have not a moment's benefit of their liberation from the over-shadowing grain, and the soil is busy at its work of summer fallowing the instant the crop is removed. In contrast, no team outfit can handle more than one process at a time. Harvesting is the big thing—the crux of the season—therefore the weeds stand from the cutting of the first swath until the last bushel of the crop is threshed and hauled.

Another vital consideration—in order to compass [*sic*] his harvest the team farmer with large acreage is forced to start cutting when his grain is a little green, and before he has finished his last field it is overripe and is beginning to drop its kernels. The horseless farmer can cut and thresh his grain when it is prime and right; the team farmer must often get a number-two grade for wheat that would have been graded number one if he could have cut and threshed it at the right moment. These claims of economics, which annually amount to thousands of dollars to farmers with large acreage in grain, seem to be supported by the farmers

who have had experience with both methods.

Also, the horseless farmer is generally able to get his seed into the ground ten days or two weeks earlier than his neighbor who must depend upon horse power—and the chances of a good yield are generally on the side of the fields that are sown early.

Other influences that are throwing the coming of the horseless age up to a high speed are the scarcity, the constantly increasing cost and the increasing inefficiency of common farm labor. Today a farmhand who plows five acres of stubble ground with a five-horse team, pulling a two-bottom gangplow, does a stiff day's work. Yet even one of the lighter tractor engines, manned by an engineer and a plow-pilot, will operate a gang of six to eight plows and break twenty acres of sod or turn twenty-five acres of stubble ground in a ten-hour day. In every operation of farming the use of the tractor greatly reduces the number of hands required.

The 1900s brought the classroom to the fields, with instruction in everything from selecting seeds to making cheese.

Working with a tractor by night is one of the very attractive possibilities of horseless farming because it enables a man, during rush seasons to do twice as much work in one twenty-four-hour period as he could otherwise accomplish. Night work with horses is not only impracticable but essentially impossible, as no farm could afford to maintain throughout the year a double force of horses in order to do night work in a special emergency.

Farming by searchlight might well be called crop insurance, because it is, in a large measure, insurance against a poor crop or a large amount of damage to a good crop. Plowing is the easiest work to do at night by searchlight because there is very little to look after behind the engine.

There are two favorite methods of illuminating for night work with the tractor. One is by means of acetylene headlights, similar to those used on automobiles. In plowing, a large headlight is placed on the front of the tractor and another on the rear to illuminate the plows. This outfit costs about fifty or sixty dollars and is generally very satisfactory.

There seems to be, however, some preference for the electric headlight. For this purpose a very powerful magneto is used—which also serves to furnish the current for the sparking device. Besides the two searchlights—on the front and the rear of the tractor—a small hand lamp is hung in the top of the canopy so that it may be moved about for the purpose of exploring the engine or other machinery. It can hardly be denied that, compared with team farming, horseless farming has the best of it, as to the investment required, the labor involved and the cost of maintenance—to say nothing of more thorough and effective work. There is no doubt among farmers who have tried both methods that the maintenance cost of keeping horses capable of doing the work of the tractor is much in excess of the operating expenses of the machine; for horses eat all the year round while the tractor eats only when it works.

There is a bigness, a swing and a spectacular charm to horseless farming that can scarcely fail to make it attractive to men who are of the sort to do big things, and to whom the old-style farming has looked petty and little. (1910)

The Magic Telephone

By WILLIAM HENRY McDONOUGH

The village of Wauseon, Ohio, had reached the conclusion that it wanted a telephone service. The business men formulated a petition, addressed to the Central Union Telephone Company. In due time there came a communication from the main office at Chicago, refusing the application. Wauseon, with less than three thousand people, was entirely too small to warrant the installation of a plant. This was in the spring of 1895.

What followed sounds like a romance. A campaign of competition was inaugurated that has revolutionized the telephone situation in the United States.

The leader was Edward L. Barber, a graduate of Cornell, head of a private banking institution inherited from his father. One of Mr. Barber's closest friends was James S. Brailey, Jr., who attended Northwestern College, the University of Cincinnati and Ohio State University, graduating as a lawyer in 1894. He had just about settled down to practice his profession in his native place when the Bell people made the foolish mistake of denying Wauseon.

Their refusal to accommodate Wauseon aroused Mr. Barber's ire. He hunted up his friend Brailey and laid the case before him. "Now," said he, "can't we compel these people to give us service?"

"No," said young Brailey, "we can't. But I'll tell you what we can do. We can get together with the other business men here and install our own system."

The two young men associated themselves then and there for the purpose of building a telephone system for the village. They didn't know anything about the business, but that didn't deter them in the least. They set to work to learn. Some other young men in the town were interested in the proposition, and one fine morning there was a central in Wauseon. There were only sixty original subscribers; to-day there are four hundred and more, or one for every seven men, women and children in the village of Wauseon.

The profit was small, but it opened the eyes of the two young men to the possibilities that lay in this line of work. They organized the Central Construction Company, a partnership concern in which they hold equal shares, and went regularly into the installation of independent telephone systems. These

young men are now the controlling factors in forty-six telephone companies in the Midwest and a few years more will see them millionaires several times over.

It is interesting to note that practically all the people who are engaged in independent telephone construction to-day were novices, men without regular training who drifted into the industry through circumstances. I doubt whether any one not actively engaged realizes what has been going on in the telephone industry during the past seven years and what may be expected in the next seven. We have only so recently emerged from the absolute domination of the Bell companies that the general public is not yet awake to the fact that there is such a thing as a first-class telephone service outside of Bell control. It will probably be news, therefore, to the public, that on the first of May there were in use in this country, in round numbers, three million four hundred thousand telephones. Of these only one million four hundred thousand were controlled by the American Bell Telephone Company, as against two million and over controlled by the independent companies.

In the past it has been the policy of the Bell Company to buy up its rivals when they showed signs of becoming formidable. But experience has shown the unwisdom of this course, for no sooner has one company been put out of business by purchase than another has sprung up. The Bell people have, therefore, practically abandoned the practice of purchasing and are meeting competition by cutting rates and improving service, a state of affairs that is bringing great joy to their subscribers.

Since 1895 more than two hundred thousand instruments have been put into farmhouses. The farmers of the Middle West have been particularly progressive. Farmers' exchanges have sprung up everywhere in Ohio, Indiana, Michigan and the neighboring States. The manner in which these exchanges go up is well illustrated by what are now known as the Stafford lines, in Geauga County, Ohio. In the spring of 1896 a number of farmers living about five miles east of Chagrin Falls, which is on the far western border of the county, concluded that it would be a pretty good thing to get into closer touch with each other by installing a telephone line running from house to house. They cut and set their own poles and here and there the fences were used to run wires. There were not over half a dozen in the original combination. The results were so satisfactory that the news spread in the neighborhood, and by fall several others concluded to build a line, using, with some extensions, the poles already erected. Up to this time it was simply possible under this scheme to talk from one house to the other. But as the number grew it was finally decided that it would be a good scheme if they could exchange conversations. One of the farmers, George W. Stafford, volunteered the use of his house as a "central" and here a switchboard was installed. Pretty soon the families in the neighborhood were fairly clamoring for connection, and as the exchange business grew Mr. Stafford realized that it would take some one's entire time to look after it. He therefore made a proposition to his neighbors to handle the exchange on a business basis. To-day this exchange, which is five or six miles away from the nearest railroad and which stands about a half mile from its nearest neighbor, controls forty-five miles of pole lines and has a hundred and fifty subscribers paying twelve dollars a year. It has a modern switchboard and its list of instruments is growing every day. It has long-distance connection with Cleveland, Painsville, Ashtabula, Warren, Youngstown and other main centres of population, besides giving free

DRAWN BY J. V. McFALL.

service throughout the entire county of Georgia.

A telephone promoter is welcomed in rural communities with more eagerness than Santa Claus. An excellent example of what may be done, is furnished by the experience of a newspaper editor at Sturgeon, Missouri. He had a country weekly, and in order to get in closer touch with his people for stock and crop reports he concluded to build a little telephone line out through a certain section, where he could tap a number of houses. His neighbors laughed at him as a scatterbrain who didn't know what to do with his money, but he kept on building. And his perseverance paid off, for he is getting the last laugh. To-day he is making more money out of his telephone line than he is out of his paper!

In 1902 telephones were used to disseminate world news—or just for some occasional "girl talk."

At Tipton, Indiana, a place of thirty-eight hundred population, forty miles from Indianapolis, there is an exchange manager who is going through the same process, only reversed. From a telephone man he is rapidly going into the field of an editor. He has a number of farm lines running out along the roads that lead to Tipton. With few exceptions, the houses along these roads are connected. The Indianapolis evening papers get into Tipton shortly after supper. The telephone man takes these papers, clips the headlines bearing on the main features, prepares a short synopsis, carefully written out, and pastes up what is known among newspaper men as a "dummy." When this is finished at a certain hour every evening he connects with all his lines, and gives a prescribed number of rings that brings every subscriber to his telephone. Then the exchange manager proceeds to read to the farmers his summary of the latest news, followed by stock reports, weather probabilities and other special information certain to interest subscribers all along the line. At the other end the news summary is received by some member of the household, who repeats it aloud to the other members of the family gathered about the telephone. In this way the farmers know the chief happenings of the world almost as soon as they occur.

Instances such as these could be multiplied by the score. People who have taken up telephony as a pastime or as a side issue have invariably ended by becoming fascinated by it and giving it their entire time. (1902) 🐚

The Age of Wireless Miracles

By SAMUEL E. MOFFETT

Guglielmo Marconi first transmitted and received signals in 1895. By 1901, he had increased the transmission range to a two-hundred-mile radius, thus launching the radio, or wireless.

If the enthusiasts on the subject of the wireless transmission of electricity were to be believed we should feel ourselves on the verge of a revolution in all the conditions of life. Telegraphing, telephoning, lighting lamps, steering torpedoes and exploding mines at a distance without wires have already been accomplished, and the inventors tell us that these things can be done hundreds and even thousands of miles away. They say that the earth is a vast reservoir of electricity, and that when we know how to tap it we can carry little instruments in our pockets and make our power felt as if by magic wands in any direction and at any distance.

But it is not necessary to believe all that these enthusiasts tell us to see that we are on the eve of great changes. The things that have already been accomplished are enough to prove that. For instance, consider the meaning of that incident at sea the other day when the *Lucania* and the *Campania* talked to each other in mid-ocean, a hundred and seventy miles

Ship-to-shore communication reduced the isolation of journeys on the sea.

apart, and a passenger on the westbound ship sent a message to a friend in Philadelphia which was transmitted from the eastbound vessel by wireless telegraphy to Ireland and thence by cable to America, enabling the Philadelphian to be at the dock in New York when his friend's ship came in.

That means that we already have a weapon that can conquer all the dangers of fogs, darkness and mistaken observations at sea. It means that in war it will be impossible for a fleet to drop out of sight, and that a hostile squadron can be traced with the help of relays of scouts from one side of the Atlantic Ocean to the other. It means that every group of islands in the world can be made a unit, as the Hawaiian group is already, without the expense of laying cables.

Draw a circle two hundred miles in diameter in the densely populated parts of the country and see what a tremendous field there is for a device that has already proved its ability to cover such an area. The revolution may not be so great as the inventors predict, but that there will be a revolution is clearly manifest. And it is already upon us. (1901)

The Speed Maniac
and the Rights of the Road

AUTHOR UNKNOWN

The automobile as a vehicle for man's daily use is here to stay. Even more permanent is its use as a vehicle for entertainment. But when a man buys an automobile the purchase does not include all the highways of the world, although in some cases he seems to think that it does. (1901)

Last week I set out for a three-days' tour in the automobile of a man I have known for years, and whom, all that time, I have believed a kindly-disposed, extremely considerate gentleman—a quality too rare to fail of making an impression when encountered. Our route lay through a succession of small towns and their suburbs on a much-traveled and unoiled highway.

We had a high-powered car and an English-speaking chauffeur; and, from the moment we left the limits of the ferry, the speed of our car was that of the racer. Evidently nothing had been made in the line of automobiles which could keep pace with us, and that every one along the dust-fogged roads should fully realize that fact was the obvious thought of the owner and his chauffeur. My dear old friend, hitherto the most regardful of men, had

been transformed into a speed maniac of the most careless type, and the chauffeur knew on which side his bread was buttered. Signs of "Slow Down" or of "Danger! Sharp Curve Ahead," or of "Reduce Speed to Ten Miles" or of "Dangerous Crossing" had no significance for us and were absolutely no brake upon our speed.

We rushed over crossroads at the rate of forty miles an hour, without sounding a horn, much less slowing down; we swirled around corners where the road narrowed, trusting to blind luck that no other maniac was coming from the opposite direction at the same pace; we whirled past pedestrians, smothering them in the dust-cloud which followed us so thickly that you could not see ten feet into it; and when we plunged into the dust-cloud of a passing car we could not see twenty feet ahead of us; but we sped on, just the same, and the only reason we did not run down some one was because, by the grace of Providence, no one chanced to be there. It was eleven o'clock in the morning when we left the ferryboat, and it was four in the afternoon when we arrived at the inn which my host had scheduled as the end of the first day's run, one hundred and fifty miles from our starting-point—an average of thirty miles an hour, including ferry, over roads none too good. And the first questions put to us by other tourists were: "Where did you come from, and what did you make it in?"

I have taken this leaf out of my book of personal experience literally as it happened, for two reasons: First, to indicate how speed mania debauches otherwise decent, law-abiding citizens, and second, to illustrate how the comfort and the lives of those living or walking or driving along roads frequented by automobile tourists are menaced. And for both of those reasons it

The 1903 Rambler and the open road—unbeatable.

seems to me that the need of an equable adjustment of rights is imperative. It is to emphasize such need that I have gone into this detail.

We are repeatedly reading in our morning newspapers, under the head of "Automobile Notes of Interest," of some one or another group of automobile owners, or club committees, that are getting together in an effort to ease some stringent State or local law affecting the speed of the automobile. And I always feel when I read this kind of thing that the interests of automobilists would be better served if effort, vigorous and sustained, was made rather to punish those who speed through the country regardless of the rights of any one, whether afoot or in a car—for the considerate drivers of automobiles also suffer at the hands of the road hog, if I may be

permitted to use that unpleasant word. Resentment of the reckless drivers' attitude has, it is true, resulted in some local regulations that are irksome, and, in some instances, nearly impossible to obey—like, for example, one regulation of which I know that limits speed to six miles the hour! There are high-powered cars which could scarcely maintain so low a speed without risk of damaging their machine, and the pace is too low for almost any kind of car, except at a likely cost to the engine. But ten miles the hour is a rate easily within the possibilities of the highest-powered machine, and from the average citizen's point of view, whether he be living along the thoroughfare or walking or driving upon it, ten miles the hour is sufficiently low to remove all danger as the car moves through the town street.

At the present, even taking into account the unjust restrictions of speed in some localities, the "average citizen" has all the worst of it. His rights are not even thought of by the average man in a car, and he is justified, in my opinion, in making such laws as will bring such people to their senses. At the moment the lid is off and we are wide open to the reckless influence of the scorcher, who speeds along the highway spreading consternation before the burr of his approaching motor and leaving a blinding dust-cloud and a trail of anathemas in his wake. With such a situation it would appear to be to the interests of all automobile clubs and automobilists generally to devote time to easing the condition of the "average citizen," instead of seeking relief from the rather just (under the circumstances) rebuff

Connecticut passed the first law regulating auto speed in 1901.

administered by certain popular touring sections.

What the automobile interest now wants is not mechanical improvement, but a more rational and more cautious and more considerate spirit among those who drive cars. Often the owner, when spoken to about the speed he has been making, will lay the blame for disregarding the rights of others upon his chauffeur, as, indeed, did my friend when, at the end of our first day (which was also my last day), I took him to task for the reckless speed we had kept up from start to finish; and that same kind of owner will, from time to time during a run, lean forward and say to the chauffeur: "Don't let that fellow give you his dust." The chauffeur does what his employer bids him, and

Driving requires utmost concentration—but seldom gets it.

he does not speed along the road regardless of every one else on the highway if his employer forbids him to do so on penalty of losing his job. It is a weak man, indeed, who is in the hands of his chauffeur; ninety-nine times out of a hundred the confession is mere subterfuge, and in the one exceptional instance a chair-car should be prescribed.

There is no doubt of there being very generally in the land a bitter feeling among residents of country towns and along country roads against automobilists; the one fact that it is unjustly comprehensive does not alter the other fact that these people have much good cause for their aversion. Such being the case, and these being the people who help to make our laws, the course of the better class of automobilists—and the better class is by far in the

majority—is plainly to work with all energy for the suppression and the punishment of the reckless and the inefficient drivers of cars. The situation demands more than half-way measures, and anything short of imprisonment for the repeatedly reckless driver, or the forfeiture of his license by the scorcher, or the seizure and withholding for a term of the car of the confederate owners, is certainly half-way arraignment. This is a case where the punishment should be made adequately to fit the crime; the ruffians who tear over the public highways unmindful of man or horse or car need legislation of the most drastic character—it cannot be too severe. And I do not a particle exaggerate the recklessness of the maniac.

The other afternoon, while going along a narrow road, I heard the hum of an approaching car, which I could not see because of the dust about it. As I never take chances when others are with me, I gave up the entire roadbed, running my car slowly, and had only just cleared when there flashed past in the middle of the road, and with such a dust-cloud all around him that the driver could not possibly see twenty feet ahead, a racer, runabout type, going at the rate of probably fifty miles an hour!

The driver was bent over the wheel, the woman with him was doubled in an effort to keep on her hat and escape the bewildering dust. If I had not got entirely off the road, no doubt there would have been coffins for several. Now, is any punishment too severe for a driver of that kind?

Around the world in 169 days! In 1908, the American Thomas Flyer *won the Great Car Race by 11 days. Sponsored by* The New York Times *and Paris'* Le Matin, *the auto earned its right to the road.*

My country home is located in a section where the farmers have become alive to the value to them of good roads, and as a result we have many splendid highways, with the farmers all prosperous, largely through the ease and cheapness of the haul to market. Also we have the sane-minded automobile tourist, and the scorcher who finds our roads delightful for his highest speed; therefore, I am in a position to see the car-driver at his worst and at his best—and scarcely a day passes that I do not either see or personally experience an encounter with some reckless creature who, if he was fittingly punished, would forthwith spend from ten to thirty days of the heated term in jail, on bread and water.

At his best, the automobilist is a considerate gentleman who slows down and sounds his horn on coming to a crossroad, who invariably notifies a driver of his approach by a small toot of the horn, who crowds neither pedestrians nor wagons into the ditch or so near to it that they are in danger of falling, who obeys the request to "slow down" and who does not shower with mud and water people he chances to have overtaken just at a pool, or confuse with his approach and dust those he may have come upon in a turn of the road. In a word, he is considerate of the rights of those he meets, and it is entirely from that viewpoint that I write.

Intelligent people do not offer objection to the speeding of automobiles, if the increased pace ceases through towns and in such roads where the request to reduce speed is made; intelligent people realize that the automobile is a great stride in methods of transportation; that, from being a luxury, it has now come almost to be a necessity; that it has come to stay, and that its requirements must be fairly considered in legislation. It is not fair to place speed limits at unnecessarily low figures; they should be put at such figures as is necessary to safeguard the ordinary traffic of the road. Once such a figure is established, however (and ten miles the hour is generally agreed to meet the sane judgment of all gentlemen), compliance should be exacted under penalty of jail, instead of under penalty of a fine, which has very little, if any, deterring effect upon the class of automobile owners that supplies the most flagrant offenders of not only local speed regulations, but of the common rules of decency.

Respect for the rights of the "average citizen" will result in respect of those of the automobilist; each needs the other. (1907)

Weapon
of the Century

By WOODS HUTCHINSON, M.D.

Scarcely more than a decade ago as the mother sat by the cradle of her first-born, musing over his future, one moment fearfully reckoning the gauntlet of risks that his tiny life had to run, and the next building rosy air-castles of his happiness and success, there was one shadow that ever fell black and sinister across his tiny horoscope. Certain risks there were which were almost inevitable—initiation ceremonies into life, mild expiations to be paid of the modern underworld, the diseases of infancy and of childhood. Most of these could be passed over with little more than a temporary wrinkle to break her smile. They were so trivial, so comparatively harmless—measles, a mere reddening of the eyelids and peppering of the throat, with a headache and purplish rash, dangerous only if neglected; chicken-pox, a child's-play at disease; scarlatina, a little more serious, but still with the chances of twenty to one in favor of complete recovery; diphtheria—ah! that drove the smile from her face and the blood from her lips. Not quite so common, not so inevitable as a prospect, but, as a possibility, full of terror, once its poison had passed the gates of the body fortress. The fight between the Angel of Life and the Angel of Death was waged on almost equal terms, with none daring to say which would be the victor, and none able to lift a hand with any certainty to aid in the struggle.

A healthy, happy child was not taken for granted in the early 1900s—anxious mothers watched fearfully for signs of dreaded childhood diseases.

It is a significant fact that the risk of developing diphtheria is greatest precisely at the age when there is not the slightest scruple about putting everything that may be picked up into the mouth, namely, from the second to the fifth year, and diminishes steadily as habits of cleanliness and caution in this regard are developed, even though no immunity may have been gained by a mild or slight attack of the disease. The tendency to discourage and forbid the indiscriminate kissing of children, and the crusade against the uses of the mouth as a pencil-holder, pincushion and general receptacle for odds and ends, would be thoroughly justified by the risks from diphtheria alone—to say nothing of tuberculosis and other infections.

For years we were in doubt as to the cause of diphtheria. Half a dozen different theories were advanced: bad sewage, foul air, overcrowding; but it was not until shortly after the discovery, by Robert Koch, of bacteriology that the germ which caused it was arrested, tried and found guilty, and our real knowledge of and control over the disease began. This was in 1883, when the bacteriologist Klebs discovered the organism, followed a few months later (in 1884) by Löffler, who made valuable additions to our knowledge of it. This put us upon solid ground and our progress was both sure and rapid; in ten years our knowledge of the causation, the method of spread, the mode of assault upon the body fortress, and last, but not least, the cure, stood out clear cut as a die, a model and a prophecy of what may be hoped for in most other contagious diseases.

The guinea-pig has been used as a stepping-stone for every inch of progress. Upon it were conducted experiments whose result widened our knowledge, until we found that this bacillus and no other would cause diphtheria; that it chiefly limited itself to growing and multiplying upon a comparatively small patch of the body surface, most commonly of the throat; that most of its serious and fatal results upon the body were produced, not by the entrance of the germs themselves into the blood, but by the absorption of the toxins or poisons produced by the germs on the moist surface of the throat.

Here was a most important clew [*sic*]. It was not necessary to fight the germs themselves, but merely to introduce some ferment or chemical substance which would have the power of neutralizing their poison. Instantly attention was turned in this direction, and it was quickly found that if a guinea-pig were injected with a very small dose of the diphtheria toxin and allowed to recover he would then be able to throw off a still larger dose until finally, after a number of weeks, he could be given a dose which would have promptly killed him in the beginning of the experiments, but which he now readily resisted and recovered from. Evidently some substance was produced in his blood which was a natural antidote for the toxin, and a little further search quickly resulted in the discovery and filtering out of his body the now famous antitoxin. A dose of this injected into another guinea-pig suffering from diphtheria would promptly save its life.

Bedside vigils were the only source of comfort the parent could provide, until the development of the antitoxin.

Could this antitoxin be obtained in sufficient amounts to protect the body of a human being? The guinea-pig was so tiny and the process of antitoxin-forming so slow that we naturally turned to larger animals as a possible source, and here it was quickly found that the horse not only would develop this antidote substance very quickly and in large amounts, but that a certain amount of it was present in his blood to begin with.

After his resisting power had been raised to the highest possible pitch by successive injections of increasing doses of the toxin, and his serum (the watery part of the blood which contains the healing body) had been used hundreds and hundreds of times to save the lives of diphtheria-stricken guinea-pigs, and had been shown over and over again not merely magically curative but absolutely harmless, it was tried with fear and trembling upon a gasping, struggling, suffocating child, as a last possible resort to save a life otherwise hopelessly doomed. Who could tell whether the "heal-serum," as the Germans call it, would act in a human being as it had upon all the other animals? In agonies of suspense, vibrating between hope and dread, doctors and parents hung over the couch. What was their delight, within a few hours, to see the muscles of the little one begin to relax, the fatal blueness of its lips to diminish, and its breathing become easier. In a few hours more the color had returned to the ashen face and it was breathing quietly. Within twenty-four hours the child was sleeping peacefully—out of danger. And the most priceless and marvelous life-saving weapon of the century had been placed in the hand of the physician. (1909) 🖋

The Times, They Are a-Changin' ...Or Are They?

An INTROSPECTIVE STUDY OF THE TIMES

The Witchery of the Weed

By WILLIAM MATHEWS

If logic and learning, satire and eloquence, could "kill off" a plant, tobacco would ages ago have ceased to be chewed, smoked or snuffed. Again and again has it been shown, by overwhelming proofs, that the tobacco habit is unthrifty, tyrannical, damaging to the health and purse; that the weed is a debilitant; that it stimulates the nerves till they become irritated nerves; that it weakens the nerve centres; that it lessens vitality, consequently energy, and renders one an easy victim to disease. Again and again has it been shown that moderation in a habit so related to the will is exceedingly difficult, because "the habit itself is one of *indulgence*, a field from which the will is shut out; and hence the only limit, ordinarily, is that imposed by satiety; the smoker stops when he does not care to smoke longer." Over all these physiological and many other potent reasons, even when their force is fully acknowledged, the witchery of the weed triumphs in the vast majority of cases and holds the smoker or chewer in a grip as fast as that which held Laocoön and his sons. (1903)

Man, creature of habit—this, for a time, a favorite indulgence.

Hard to Swallow

An EDITORIAL

Government chemists in the food laboratory at Washington have been subjecting American jams, jellies and preserved fruits to analysis. The discoveries made are astounding.

Of two hundred and fourteen samples of fruit products one hundred and four were found to be adulterated.

Crystals of acid tartrate of potash were discovered in plum jam. In many samples of jellies benzoic acid and salicyclic acid had been used as preservatives. But that was not the worst feature. As permanent color is an important item in the sale of fruit products, some manufacturers had used poisonous dyes. As a result small quantities of zinc, lead, arsenic and other dangerous impurities had been imparted to some very attractive looking jellies.

The Government will circulate a list of the two hundred and fourteen brands examined, giving the name of the manufacturers, the claims of purity made for the product, and the disclosures of the Federal laboratory. (1903)

The Craze for Health

An EDITORIAL

This new excitement and enthusiasm over health is often spoken of as a fad—like angel sleeves and roller-skating and pigs-in-clover—something that is sweeping through the country to blow out to the sea of oblivion and be heard of no more. But is it?

Science has made life vastly more comfortable than it used to be. It has opened up infinitely greater possibilities of greater comfort. It is teaching men and women how they can live long in

the strength, beauty and joy of health. Is not the so-called fad merely another instance of human shrewdness and swiftness in seizing upon a "good thing"?

Artificial lighting at once became a fad—and has remained a fad steadily ever since. The craze for betterment is one that will die only with the race. (1904) 🐾

Fine Thinking
An EDITORIAL

Having been found guilty of rebating on nearly fifteen hundred counts by a Federal trial jury at Chicago, the Standard Oil Company may be forced to pay fines aggregating almost thirty-three million dollars.

Indictments have been returned in other districts. If the court at Chicago imposes the maximum punishment, and its action is not overturned on some technicality in the various appeals that are sure to follow, the defendant will no doubt arrange to finance all possible fines in a lump. We should, in that event, expect to see an issue of Standard Oil Company Fine Equalization Debentures, to be secured by a trust indenture which would provide that, to the price of every gallon of kerosene or other product of petroleum sold by the company during the life of the debentures, there should be added the sum of two cents, to be turned over to the trustees for the debenture holders and by them held until the amount was sufficient to pay off and retire

all of the company's outstanding debentures.

Such debentures would be a first-class security, readily marketable. For twenty years the Standard Oil Company has controlled the price of petroleum and its products, and to-day is unquestionably in a position to collect from the users of petroleum any fines that may be assessed against it—as easily as the hard-coal combine reimbursed itself for increased wages. Fining a monopoly is nothing more, in the final outcome, than fining the people who use the monopolized product. (1907) 🐾

Petticoat Professionals
By DR. WALTER E. WEYL

A new type is arising in American society—the wife who works for wages. It is no novelty for wives to work; they have always labored.

But formerly the wife was simply a housewife toiling at home for the home folks. Now she has left her home to search the business world for a job. A million wives have already taken their places in American industry, and their number is constantly increasing.

A million wives earning their own living—a vital fact, this! Nothing could be more important, more far-reaching. The great political events of this era that loom large in the public mind—the struggle for tariff reform, for rate regulation, for municipal ownership—all these pale

On her own.

into insignificance beside this fundamental development in the life of the American wife. A million wives laboring for money cannot but leave an impress upon wife and husband and the child, upon home and factory, upon society in general. (1907) 🐾

Haste Makes Waste

By JUDGE MARCUS KAVANAGH

Marriage is not such a serious or permanent matter, after all," the law assures the citizen. In half of the divorce cases tried in the Chicago courts during the present year the marital relation had not existed for more than three years. It is safe to assert that the very idea of the permanence of the relationship in many of these instances was absent at the time of the wedding ceremony itself. All unformed and unshaped it may have been, but on the day the marriage ceremony was performed, in the minds of the contracting parties lingered the knowledge that the union was not necessarily for life.

If a married couple can weather through the disillusions and troubles of the first five or six years, their chances of spending their lives together may be considered fairly good. This chance is greatly enhanced by the presence of children; however, the ease with which divorce can be obtained under the law militates against the general stability of the marital relation.

This last generalization seems to call for more serious concern than either of the others, because it is from this general knowledge of the ease with which divorce may be obtained that so many hasty marriages result. And in these hasty marriages lies the heart of the evil. (1905) 🐾

The Legal Bind

An EDITORIAL

None who gives attention to the matter will deny that this country would be freer and happier if there were a lawful check against laws. This lack has resulted in such a mass of restraints that not the lawyers themselves keep track of them. It cannot be that so many measures are needed to preserve the uprightness of a country that is naturally as upright as any in the world, yet it is a fact that over 20,000 pages of laws issue every year from the legislatures.

We live in a riot of law making. It is a blessing that most of the measures are dead letters from the day of their enactment, yet it is a danger that any of them can be resurrected from the limbo of the forgotten and used to enforce an unjust demand or express a prejudice.

One could multiply the absurdities and inconsistencies for which zeal in law making is responsible, but it would not check their increase. That is best prevented by allowing the people to approve or nullify their laws. Initiative and referendum offer great possibilities, for if laws were submitted for final adoption to the people themselves, or, if we could confine our legislatures to biennial performances of not more than sixty days' duration, there would be a surcease of law, and the governing statutes would sift down to a few sensible measures. We elect men to make laws, but men who would unmake hundreds now on the books should be hurried into office by tumultuous majorities. (1901) 🐾

The Judge at the City Gate

By ROBERT SHACKLETON

Alas for the passing of the judge who sat at the city gate! In the olden day justice was prompt and expeditious. As civilization has grown swifter justice has grown slower; as marvelous rapidity has been attained in the practical progress of the world, justice has grown more laggard. We need the quick decision of the judge who sat at the gate of the city—the judge who is ready to pass promptly on whatever case shall come before him.

There was a directness about the old-fashioned way. Cases were decided out of hand, and there was fully as great a chance of securing substantial justice as under the present long-drawn-out system. There were mistakes and injustice, of course, but no more than there are now.

In criminal cases there is often a most harmful delay. A man is arrested, charged with a great crime, and then months and months may pass before he is brought to trial, and weeks and weeks spent in the hearing, long after the witnesses have forgotten their clear impressions of what they saw and knew. And then, more than likely, a new trial is granted, and the farce is solemnly played out again. It is an outrage upon the prisoner, upon the public, or upon both.

Our twentieth century, with its boasted swiftness in all but justice, would do well to secure in that the prompt readiness of the judge who sat at the gate of the city. (1902) 🐝

Breathing Space

By HONORÉ PALMER

In a big city, the wholesome pleasures of childhood are limited and circumscribed, even for the children of the wealthy; for those of the poor they are pitiably meagre, cramped, barren and sordid; devoid of all that is calculated to awaken the finer sensibilities and nourish the more wholesome activities of the mind and heart.

Thus the question: What means are best adapted to modify, from the viewpoint of the city child, this oppressive legacy of metropolitan sordidness? Undoubtedly the public playground, in the heart of the congested tenement district, is the foremost agency in the field. Next to this ranks the small park or "breathing space." Without either of these breaks

in the grim encroachment of brick and stone, the playspots of the children must become daily more circumscribed until the natural rendezvous of city children, the vacant lot, entirely disappears, and they have left only the bare pavement and the large park. The most densely populated city districts are generally somewhat remote from the large public parks. More than this, the children are in large measure shut out from the big public parks because they cannot afford the carfare. Some, it is true, indulge in the luxury of a Sunday pilgrimage to them, but more spend their entire childhood in the immediate neighborhood of their tenements. (1901) 🐝

Checks and Balances

By EMERSON HOUGH

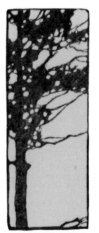

DRAWN BY EMLEN McCONNELL

The American standard of living is based on the theory of an exhaustless bank account. Our account has never been overdrawn, and we have never had our bankbook balanced. It is only now that a few of our wiser men begin to see that it is time for us to get a balance from the clerk at the desk. We have been checking out, like inebriated mariners, what we had or thought we had in this rich bank of America, land of the free, country of endless opportunity. Now we have used up our forests, are exhausting our mines at fearsome speed, have exterminated most of our wild game, endangered the food supply which comes from the waters,

and, in general, done all we could to put an end to our great resources, spending both our interest and our principal. Not only are we using up the natural products of the soil, but we are also using up *the soil itself*.

We don't own the soil. We borrow it. We ought to hand it over to our successors in as good condition as when we asked the loan.

The time has come for a showdown between the American people and America itself. (1909) 🐝

The Illustrations

The many illustrations used throughout this book are taken almost exclusively from issues of the *Post* dating from 1901 to 1910. The two-color art is, in most instances, a cover, or, as in a few cases, an ad which appeared on the inside of the cover. The black-and-white art is from the interior of the magazine, which at that time was printed entirely in black-and-white.

Since they do not reproduce well, no photographs were used in this book, though they were used in the *Post* during this decade.

Each illustration is listed below by the page number on which it appears, and as it appears (going from left to right and top to bottom), in this book. The artist (if known) is identified for each, along with the date of the issue in which it was published. The source of those pieces of art not from the *Post* is also indicated. 🍂